Praise for
The Measure of a

D0546663

"As an experienced radio current affairs producer, JJ Lee knew what it took to make a good story though he never expected his own life to end up in a book. . . . Beautifully crafted, Lee's memoir is a heartbreaking page-turner about a family, an abusive father, and men's fashion. Who could have thought these themes could work together? In his first book, Lee has shown us how." – Jury citation, Charles Taylor Prize for Literary Non-Fiction

"A story about self-fashioning, about taking what you have been given, or have been left, and of making the best of it. In *The Measure of a Man*, JJ Lee has made something very good indeed." – Andre Gerard, editor of *Fathers: A Literary Anthology*

"Touching and inquisitive . . . [A] striking and accomplished blend of humour, information and pathos. . . . [A] thoughtful and intermittently provocative memoir." – *National Post*

"[*The Measure of a Man*] hangs on the device of a son trying to alter his late father's suit to fit himself. It's an elegant way to stitch together several subjects. . . . A deftly crafted memoir. . . ." – Montreal *Gazette*

"In his often heartbreaking yet humorous and compelling memoir, Lee reveals a story that centres around his father, once a successful restaurateur with a closet full of beautifully tailored suits, who slowly loses his battle with alcoholism." – *Calgary Herald*

"Lee's book skillfully weaves a personal struggle to understand his estranged father after his death through the process of repurposing his dad's suit to fit his smaller frame. . . . Truly inspires." – *Gear Patrol*

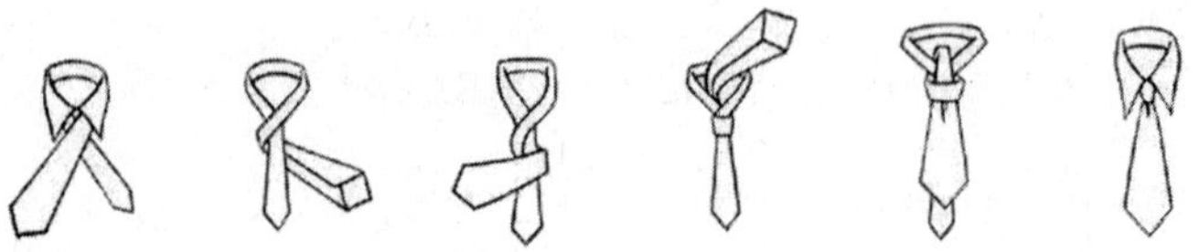

The Measure of a Man

- - - - -

THE STORY OF A FATHER, A SON, AND A SUIT

JJ Lee

EMBLEM
McCLELLAND & STEWART

Cloth edition published 2011
Emblem edition published 2012

Emblem is an imprint of McClelland & Stewart,
a division of Random House of Canada Limited

Emblem and colophon are registered trademarks of McClelland & Stewart,
a division of Random House of Canada Limited

LIBRARY AND ARCHIVES CANADA CATALOGUING IN PUBLICATION

Lee, J. J. (James-Jason)
The measure of a man : the story of a father, a son, and a suit / JJ Lee.

Includes bibliographical references.
ISBN 978-0-7710-4648-3

1. Lee, J. J. (James-Jason) 2. Tailors–British Columbia–Vancouver– Biography.
3. Journalists–British Columbia–Vancouver–Biography. 4. Fathers and sons–Biography.
5. Suits (Clothing)–History. 6. Suits (Clothing)–Social aspects.
7. New Westminster (B.C.)–Biography.
I. Title.

TT505.L44A3 2012   646.40092   C2012-900638-6

We acknowledge the financial support of the Government of Canada through
the Canada Book Fund and that of the Government of Ontario through the Ontario
Media Development Corporation's Ontario Book Initiative. We further acknowledge
the support of the Canada Council for the Arts and the Ontario Arts Council
for our publishing program.

Published simultaneously in the United States of America by McClelland & Stewart,
a division of Random House of Canada Limited,
P.O. Box 1030, Plattsburgh, New York 12901

Library of Congress Control Number: 2012931610

Typeset in Joanna by M&S, Toronto
Printed and bound in Canada

McClelland & Stewart,
a division of Random House of Canada Limited
75 Sherbourne Street
Toronto, Ontario
M5A 2P9
www.mcclelland.com

1   2   3   4   5   16   15   14   13   12

To sons who still need their fathers
and fathers who still need their sons

GOD IS IN THE DETAILS.

MIES VAN DER ROHE, ARCHITECT

WE DON'T WORK IN QUARTER INCHES. WE'RE NOT ENGINEERS.

WILLIAM WONG, MASTER TAILOR

THERE IS A SUIT IN THE BACK OF MY CLOSET. OVER the years dust has gathered on its shoulders. I own other, better suits but I hold on to this one because, for me at least, it is special.

The suit attracts and repels me. It came to me under the saddest of circumstances, and I've dared to wear it in public only once. I wore it to test myself, to see if it would fit – not only in its cut and dimensions, but to prove to myself I could bear the mantle and wear it without feeling like an impostor, a boy posing as a man. Most of the time I try to ignore it, and so years can go by without my touching it. But even so, I always know it's there.

Once in a while, I feel compelled to run my hand along its lapels and think of the man who wore it. I see the line of his jaw, his broad torso and its incipient roundness. I see the pores on his fleshy, bulbous nose. I remember the feel of his thick skin and the dryness of his hands, and I wonder if I look like him.

This is my father's suit.

The coat is single-breasted with a notch lapel. A boy would say it is black; in fact, it is dark navy. I lift the hanger off the rod and turn the suit this way and that in the morning sun breaking through the blinds. When the angle is just right, the colour has more depth than I remember, flashing with casts of royal and cerulean blue. Perhaps it is only my imagination, or a trick of the light.

Even without putting the jacket on, I can tell it won't fit me, although I have grown heavier and thicker over the years. The chest is too full and the shoulders are too wide. My father was always the bigger man, but the exaggerated proportions are as much a by-product of dated tastes as the measuring tape. The button placement is low and swaying, evidence of Giorgio Armani's early louche influence on menswear. It has been decades since it was considered stylish to button jackets below the natural belt line (think of the days of *Miami Vice*). Contemporary fashion dictates the crucial fastening point must be closer to the sternum, far above the belly button. (The higher "button stance" creates the illusion of longer legs.) In nearly every detail – the broad shoulders, the low notch on the wide lapel, the two heavy brass buttons hanging at a low, testicular altitude – the suit is old, outmoded.

Why does it matter? If it doesn't fit, why not throw the suit out and buy a new one?

Outside of a Konica camera he gave me as a wedding present and a pair of metal eyeglass frames I found in his apartment after his death, this suit is the only thing I have from my father. Though I have been tempted to abandon it by the back door of the Salvation Army store down the hill, the suit won't let me.

A suit is never just a suit.

Whether one wears them regularly or not, suits elicit strong reactions. If you are feeling oppressed, you might call your oppressor a "suit." If you choose to face your oppressor head on, you might want to get "suited up." A suit can be a form of armour; it can also be a form of confinement.

For my father, wearing a suit helped him declare his manhood to the world. He became a parent and breadwinner at the age of eighteen, during the late Sixties, a time when his peers were challenging the establishment and many of them wouldn't have been caught dead in a suit. My father, who as a young man rose quickly in the restaurant business in Montreal, embraced suits to ward off the impression of being out of his depth. He needed to appear older, wiser, and more competent than perhaps he was. Later on, when he felt more secure in his accomplishments, suits became a pleasure, or so I believed for most of my life.

As the suit has evolved over the last four centuries – moving from the tailcoat and morning coat (both short in the front and long in the back) to the long-skirted frock coat (imagine Abraham Lincoln) to the lounge suit (essentially our modern-day suit) – it has accumulated layers of meaning, signifying different things to different people at different times. The suit has baggage. It carries the weight of male history and shifting ideas of manhood and father-hood, success and failure, class and beauty.

My father's suit is simply a coat matched to a pair of pants, yet it is a highly articulate form of dress. I can add a shirt, tie, and pocket square to the ensemble, and the suit becomes a haiku of who I am or wish to be for that day: handsome, dangerous, serious, modern, quirky (if I add a bow tie), unforgettable. The suit, however, also speaks in a manner beyond my complete control. I may think I look one way but others will see me differently. It can't be helped. The suit has the ability to summon the unbidden and liminal; it has an X-factor, a mojo. It's one of the qualities that make the suit so appealing and explains why it has endured the test of time.

In the early days of their evolution, suits were considered rebellious: seventeenth-century Protestant clergy pining for the days of long robes and modest tunics that covered a man's legs and disguised the anatomical differences between the sexes wrote treatises attacking the sin of wearing suits. In our own time, the suit has become the dress of the establishment. All sorts of fashion revolutionaries and resistors have attempted to bring about the death of the suit, but so far none have succeeded. The acceptance of jeans as appropriate casual wear in the 1950s delivered a blow. So did the explosion of sportswear in the 1970s. Then there is the slow eroding tide of casual Fridays, which, through inspired campaigns by Dockers and The Gap, have now spread throughout the entire week. But this is the ebb and flow of fashion. The suit still stands as the sine qua non of menswear. In fact, the suit is witnessing a renaissance.

But what really gives the suit its power? What makes so many men (and a good number of women too) choose to embrace its ubiquity and authority?

What do I want from my father's suit?

Standing between the hamper and the foot of the bed with his jacket in my hands, I sink my face into the wool and breathe in his scent for the first time in years.

In *A Natural History of the Senses* Diane Ackerman writes, "Nothing is more memorable than a smell. One scent can be unexpected, momentary and fleeting, yet conjure up a childhood summer beside a lake in the mountains; another, a moonlit beach; a third, a family dinner of pot roast and sweet potatoes during a myrtle-mad August in a Midwestern town. Smells detonate softly in our memory like poignant land mines hidden under the weedy mass of years. Hit a trip-wire of smell and memories explode all at once. A complex vision leaps out of the undergrowth."

In my memory, I am seven and enthralled by my father's suits. I visit them when he is at work. In my parents' bedroom I grab the slatted folding closet doors and fling them open. The suits are hanging in a perfect row, like Spartan hoplites. Flannels. Pinstripes. Grey double-breasteds. Silk and mohair sports jackets with white buttons. Three-piece affairs thumping with the music of Abba and Boney M. They are made-to-measure and custom. A label hand-sewn into the lining promises it is "Exclusively tailored for John H. Lee." I say the phrase over and over to myself – a mantra. The wood hangers are stamped in gold letters: *A. Gold and Sons. Holt Renfrew.*

To me, these suits mean going out into the world and having adventures. They mean being a man, being formidable. They mean cigarettes and Johnny Walker Red and knowing every maître d' and floor manager in every high-end restaurant and lounge in downtown Montreal.

The house is quiet. With my arms spread wide, I turn my cheek and lean into his jackets, and it feels like I am falling into a dense but soft thicket. The suits push back in perfect unison. For a moment I'm suspended in air, and then I slip to the closet floor onto his dirty dress shirts, dragging a couple of the coats down with me. At the bottom, there is the smell of wool and of him, the scent of cigarettes, sweat, and the faint hint of vanilla.

Now, here I am more than three decades later, in my bedroom, still hanging on.

I put the jacket on. In the mirror, I see it is too wide in the shoulders. The lapels make me look heavy and squat. The pant pleats do not help. I feel old and tired in them, as he had become. His failures become mine, as if they have accreted into the wool. But I also see potential. For all the suit's faults, I can see new lines and silhouettes.

I know I can't change my father or the things he did. But maybe with a seam ripper and a pair of scissors I can alter this, his last suit. Yes, it may prove a disaster. I may screw up and this part of him will disappear forever. Maybe that's exactly what I want. But maybe, if I am patient and unravel the threads with care, the suit will give up its story to me. My father's story.

I am not totally untrained for this project. I am merely undertrained. My complicated background in tailoring began nine years ago, with my father's funeral. I wore a grey suit with a shirt-styled ghillie collar that I had bought earlier from Mexx, and which I grew to hate once I was made aware of its many deficiencies. But I owned nothing else. To this day I am ashamed of the way I dressed for my father. My sense of inadequacy grew to the point where I even skipped going to my convocation when I graduated from architecture school because I had nothing to wear. My master's degree came in the mail.

That's when I decided something had to be done. I went to Modernize Tailors. Established in 1913 and now run by octogenarian brothers Bill and Jack Wong, this venerable shop is the last of its kind in Vancouver's Chinatown. Bill made me my first made-to-measure suit back in 2001, four months after my father died. Then he made me his special project. He taught me about the craft of tailoring and about the dignity of wearing a suit. He became a father figure to me. Now he is my master tailor and I am his apprentice.

Though it may be years before I am allowed to make a suit in the shop, there's nothing to prevent me from altering my father's suit at home. I do have one thing going for me. Bill says I have a good eye.

And my eye tells me I need to change the notch of my father's suit. The notch — the point where the collar steps down to meet the lapel — is below the clavicle and far below the level of a tie knot, which creates clumsy proportions on a short man like myself.

This then will be the launching point from where I will roam across the surface of my father's suit and claim all that lies before me, making it my own. I will map its terrain; lapels, notches, side pockets, buttons, sleeves, side seams, and vents will be its features. Some I will alter. Others I will leave alone. And maybe, like a construction crew trying to get a job done in Jerusalem, I will stumble upon the ruins of my father and they will tell me something about our downfall, the tumult he brought upon himself, our family, and me.

There were times in my life when I believed he was the greatest dad in the world, and other times when I wished the scrape of the key against the lock late at night was only a bad dream. But it wasn't a dream. It was my father.

$$\bigwedge$$

It is 1978. I am eight years old. We are living in Saint-Lambert, Quebec. The basement TV is on. A football game, most likely the Alouettes. Outside it is warm, but down here it is cool. My father is taking a nap on the couch.

I work some space for myself on the couch and I curl up to him, listening to him inhale and exhale under the murmur of the play-by-play. He draws breath in deeply but the pattern is ragged. He smokes two packs of Belmont Milds a day.

I am afraid he won't wake up. That he will exhale one final time and nothing will follow. So I breathe for him. His breath breaks and I hold mine for what feels like ten seconds and a thousand years. Suddenly he draws in.

I try to synchronize our rhythms. If I breathe, he breathes.

In the tight knot of our limbs – his left arm under my head, the right pulling me in, one of my cold feet shoved between his legs for warmth – he embraces me even tighter until I fall asleep.

Against this, how can a judgment be rendered? What measure can be taken?

I HAVE FEW PICTURES OF MY FATHER, JOHN HING
Foon Lee, as a child. One of the earliest shows my father
standing in a backyard with his paternal grandparents and
his older brother, Jim. My father wears a thick cardigan with
contrast ribbing and a bow tie. He is no older than eight.

All the photographs from my father's childhood are like
this. He is invariably dressed in a tie. Sometimes he wears a
suit. The photographs were intended for his parents back in
China, who had sent him to Canada as a four-year-old to live
with his grandparents. My father never saw his mother again.
I was never told why. The dressy photographs, I suppose,
were meant to reassure his parents that they had made the
right choice.

I have even fewer facts about his early life. My father
often told me, "Your great-grandfather used to beat the hell
out of me. You're lucky if I just give you a spanking." (He rarely
did; just hoisting me over his lap and raising his hand was
enough to make me bawl.)

These are the only other details I have: he lived with his grandparents in Sherbrooke, a small town serving the farms tucked among the rolling hills of Quebec's Eastern Townships. There, they ran a laundry. My father attended a school run by Jesuits, who also used to beat him. It may have been the beatings or it may have been the urge to escape poverty that forced my father to head out on his own at the age of thirteen. He found work as a waiter at a Chinese restaurant called the Dragon Room in Chomedey, a rural suburb north of Montreal. He lived in a room above the restaurant. That's where he met my mother, Shui Kum Chang, when they were both fifteen years old.

The Dragon Room was owned by Montgomery Chang, the man who would become my maternal grandfather, and his uncle, Stanley. Montgomery had immigrated to Canada in 1956 to establish a foothold in Quebec before sending for his family. When the permits came through, my grandmother and her four children, including my mother, flew in from Hong Kong to reunite with Montgomery and start a new life in Canada. One of the first things the family did when they arrived in Canada was visit the Dragon Room.

The day my father met my mother is a day he never forgot. It was December 7, 1964. Snow was blowing outside. He saw her walk into the restaurant cold and shivering. My mother didn't yet own a coat. He noticed her tweed skirt suit with the hem above the knee and her high heels. He also noticed her legs. I am told he stared, which is forgivable. My father was the youngest person working at the Dragon Room and possessed very little guile. All the other waiters teased him, "That's the girl for you."

It wasn't a joke to my father. He told them all, "I'm going to marry her."

When the time came for my mother and her family to leave, Montgomery instructed my father to show them the way home – a duplex less than a mile away.

From then on, whenever my mother came by the restaurant it was always my father who volunteered to take her home. Their conversations were limited. My father spoke English, French, and the Chinese dialect of Toisanese, but my mother only spoke Cantonese. Mostly, they walked in silence. My father was already in love.

Then in the summer of 1965, during one of their walks, they were caught by a thunderstorm and ran back to the house. It was empty. The rest of the family was still at the restaurant. My father and mother stripped off their clothes and made love for the first time.

According to my mother, "He had claimed me from the start. There was no one else."

I have a picture of my father from a few years later, during what I call his *Rebel Without a Cause* period. His hair is swept up in a pompadour just like James Dean's. He's wearing a red windbreaker with the embroidered provincial emblems of British Columbia and Alberta sewn onto his sleeve. It was a badge of his worldliness, proof of a cross-country trip. He may have been just a teen but he had experienced something of the world.

What always catches my eye is how the sleeves of his jacket drape and fall exactly to the crook of his wrists, the perfect length. I also see he is a work in progress. Even then he liked clothes and was searching for how clothes could make the man. I see his ambition.

He believed he had to make money to be my mother's one true love. At the age of sixteen, she had long black hair, dark smooth skin, and strong, high cheekbones. She was impetuous and socially unguarded. She didn't drink, she didn't smoke, but she was the wild one. She was beautiful. When my mother entered grade ten in the fall of 1966, my father made sure she was the only girl at school wearing a diamond engagement ring.

A year later my mother was pregnant with my older sister, Tammy. Exactly a month after Tammy's birth, my father married my mother. Ten months after their wedding I was born.

By the time my father was nineteen, he was married with two kids, and his family was living above a diner on Sherbrooke Street in Notre-Dame-de-Grâce. He had no education, no real skills. He was now working as a busboy at Ruby Foo's, a Chinese restaurant frequented by the wealthy and the famous. But my father was a keen observer. He took note of the style and manners of the customers and began to emulate them. He was handsome. He dressed exceedingly well. He moved with athletic grace. When a job opened up at the illustrious Kon-Tiki Polynesian Restaurant, housed in the elegant Sheraton Mount Royal Hotel, he worked as a busboy for one week before he was promoted to host.

In my father's mind, big love and big ambition went hand in hand. He wanted it all.

IF YOU WALK BY THE SHOP, IT ALWAYS LOOKS CLOSED. From the outside it seems to be in a deep mercantile hibernation. There is no way anyone conducts any sort of business inside. Not to say it looks abandoned, just fallow, somehow lost in the timestream. The shop resides on the ground floor of a narrow brick building no wider than twenty-five feet across. The bricks have started to flake and they might crumble entirely if you poked at them hard with a stick. Even with the lights on, the cluttered storefront windows, the water-stained ceiling tiles, the flaking gold-leaf letters on the glass announcing "Modernize Tailors" all suggest that if you try the door, you will find it locked. But it won't be.

Along the walls inside are hundreds of bolts of fabric that belong in a museum. Wardrobe designers often come in to buy fabric if they're working on a period piece. In the centre of the shop is the cutting table. Most of the work here is made-to-measure: existing pattern blocks are laid out and traced with tailor's soap, a white waxy bar, onto four yards of wool. The lines are then adapted to fit the specific customer, and then the cutter, either Bill or Jack Wong, will cut out the pieces that will make up the suit. At the back of the shop is the workbench. This is where the sewing, steaming, pounding, and muttered Cantonese swearing take place. Bill, Jack, Park, and Laddie each have their own spot on the bench. I don't.

I'm allowed in the back only when one of the tailors is away. If I use a spot on the workbench, I have to pick up all the threads and scraps. I am to leave nothing behind.

In fact, if you were to come into the store when I'm there, you would likely trip over me. When I sew, I use the sewing machine right by the front door: a black 1904 Singer foot-powered treadle machine converted to work with an electric motor. Not the best machine for a beginner, but it's my own fault.

You see, I lied when I told Bill Wong I could sew.

I had to when I signed on to be an apprentice at Modernize Tailors. The tailors were old and busy and didn't really have time for an apprentice. But by that time I had been hanging around the shop for years, and they knew I loved the place, so they agreed to take me on even though, at thirty-seven, I was too old to learn the trade. Most apprentices start between the ages of fourteen and seventeen, when the fingertips are still sensitive enough to do needlework by touch, the way Bill still does. Good touch is an indispensable trait for a tailor, more so than good eyes. In fact, the blind tailor is a common stock character in literature. In one fairy tale by the Brothers Grimm, a blind

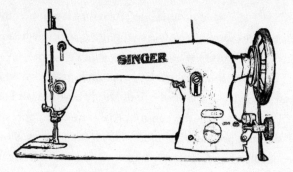

tailor can mend together anything with his magical needle and thread, even a chasm between two lands. Literary metaphors aside, a tailor with an excellent sense of touch can overcome the limitations of poor lighting. In eighteenth- and nineteenth-century surveys of the hardships of the labouring class, correspondents often reported discovering blind tailors working in dismal sweatshops with no ventilation or lighting. (In Gothic short stories, the hero would often turn a corner in some alley and stumble upon blind tailors in a dim basement.)

These days electricity makes a total dependence on touch unnecessary, but tailors still need to feel their way through the work even if it's on a machine. So I lied to my master tailor when I told Bill Wong I could hand-sew. I had gone to art and architecture school and had of course learned how to draft. Both skills require adept hand-eye control, so I assumed I'd find using a sewing machine a snap. Really, how hard could it be?

During my first official week as an apprentice, Bill sat me down in front of the old Singer and gave me a scrap of wool to test my skills.

"Sew me a set of parallel lines, then turn it around ninety degrees and show me you can stop the machine when you reach a line. I don't want to see one stitch go over."

I lifted the foot, placed the scrap underneath, rolled the hand wheel to set the needle in the ready position, and then I put my weight on the control pedal. I tried to apply only the slightest pressure. The motor began to turn over. Slowly the needle marched down a line. My hands were in the wrong position and the stitches started to veer to the right.

"Good. You shouldn't pull at it. Let the machine do the work. Just guide it."

I made the machine advance a few more stitches.

"I thought you said you could sew?"

"I just need to get used to the machine. It's very sensitive."

"It's just like driving a car, working the motor with the pedal."

"I don't know how to drive."

"Okay. You just push on the pedal gently and then let it speed up. Everything will be okay."

Even though the motor on the Singer was nearly one hundred years old, it is capable of reaching 1,500 RPM when it is well serviced. This one was. The needle flashed up and down and the feed dog turned out to be a pit bull. The machine grabbed the scrap out of my hands and flung it off the table.

"Golly," said Bill. "You better practise."

He shooed me out of the seat and slipped in. "See, you have to have control. You should be able to make the machine do anything. Watch my knee. I control the foot pressure. That way I can go backwards or sideways."

He moved his hands in small circles, the needle flashing and dancing at his whim. When he was done, he handed the scrap back to me. In perfect cursive over-stitching he had written, "JJ Learn to Sew."

I first met Bill in 2001, a few months after my father's death, and shortly after I was supposed to collect my graduate degree in architecture. The preceding years had been a struggle, a dark time filled with heartsickness, secret poverty, academic probation, and near suicide.

In the summer of 1994, as I was about to start my first year in architecture school, I met a woman who decided she was bisexual just long enough for me to fall in love with her. I spent the rest of that academic year reeling from the breakup. By the end of the second semester, I was broke, depressed, and, in truth, suicidal. After spending seventy-two hours straight in the wood shop, trying to complete an architectural model, I presented my year-end project and then threw my drawings, pencils, drafting squares, and the model into the trash. I went AWOL from school.

I ended up on welfare, living in a rummy hotel in Vancouver's Gastown district. My room was ten feet by ten feet. I painted the walls, ceiling, and floor yellow and slept on a bed I made out of shipping pallets and pieces of wood I found in an alley. Although I didn't drink or use drugs like some of the other tenants, I felt I belonged there. I was useless to the world and felt no one would miss me if I died.

This is a dangerous thought. It is the kind of thought that led me to buy two bottles of sleeping pills and a quart of bourbon, and made me sit at the edge of my bed and ask, "Do I really want to do this?"

The answer was no. I called Shannon, one of the most important people in my life, and when I saw her face, afraid, bewildered, pleading, I had to confront my own self-ishness and narcissism.

In retrospect, if I were to boil things down, I would say I simply survived a phase. It was like a hormonal problem, but in my brain. Whatever hormones make young men want to be reckless, fight, kill, and wage wars made me want to kill myself. The pressure dissipated and, over time, the effects began to subside and I outgrew depression.

Gradually, incrementally, I rebuilt myself over the course of the next year. I found a job at a photographic arts gallery. My responsibilities were to watch the gallery shop and, when the exhibition preparator was willing, paint walls, cut mattes, and mount photographs. There was no real dress code, a good thing because I looked like hell. Up to that point in my life I had fully rejected everything my father represented – the suits, the cars, the need to wear a nice watch, or to show off in any material way. I was post-grunge. I shaved my head. I wore plaid shirts and army boots with engineer's overalls from Army and Navy.

Then I got my first paycheque. While most of it went to food and rent, I spent $25 to buy a tie. It had blue, yellow, and white stripes, and the blades were broad. I started wearing it to work. I used the only tie knot I knew at the time, the one my father taught me when I was ten.

Whenever I tie it, it's like I'm ten years old again. I am standing in front of the bathroom mirror. My father is behind me and guiding my hands, his hands clasped over mine. To tie a half-Windsor, you loop the tie once around, crossing it through the neck hole, and then you loop it again. The cross and extra loop thicken the knot but not as much as it would on the full Windsor. I suppose an instructional diagram would be very helpful here, but it would fail to convey the heat and thickness of my father's hands and how I stood up on tiptoe so I could feel the rasp of his chin stubble against the back of my neck. A diagram would say nothing of the crisp frictions of woven silk, or the firm final tug – drawn with a violent mixture of humour and malevolence only fathers can offer – that rocked me onto the balls of my feet. A tie never felt so solid and lush and full and fundamental. It may have been the last moment of close physical contact I had with my father without any self-consciousness.

I wore the half-Windsor with my striped overalls, army boots, and shaved head. That's how I looked when I met Melissa of Melbourne, Australia. She was touring Canada when she walked into the gallery and into my life wearing blue leggings, Doc Martens, a poodle skirt, and a cotton blouse with lace on the collar. A year later, we were married.

I went back to architecture school and graduated five years later. Kind of.

I never wore a graduation gown or a tasselled cap. No one shook my hand or passed me a vellum scroll with "Master of Architecture" inscribed on it. I didn't go to my convocation. Even though I knew I had earned my degree, I just couldn't make myself attend the graduation ceremony. My excuse was a classic: I had nothing to wear.

I did own two suits but they were poor specimens. One was an ugly green suit I had bought for a job interview as a weight-loss counsellor. The other was the grey ghillie suit. It had four buttons; normal suits have only two or three. The pants had denim-styled pockets instead of the slash or seam pockets of more formal dress pants. The suit jacket had a horizontal seam at the back called a yoke; real suits usually have a vertical one. This suit was made of viscose; real suits are supposed to be made of wool. When I bought it for an awards dinner I had to attend at the behest of an employer, I was unaware of these deficiencies, these violations. To me it looked like a regular suit. I had no idea it was a bastard garment, a mutant and a failure, until a woman at the awards ceremony observed (was it sarcasm?), "I like your suit. It looks like something young men would wear in Shanghai."

I felt as if she had thrown a drink in my face. Her words stung. I'm sure they were intended as a compliment but somehow they felt backhanded. Did I detect an unconscious ethnic slur? What did Shanghai have to do with anything? The reference to my age: was I out of my depth? Perhaps I was the problem. I was unaccustomed to wearing a suit and felt self-conscious. In truth, I was wearing a costume. The suit wasn't really me.

This was not the way a suit was supposed to work. Later on, in my journey to better understand sartorial matters, I would speak to menswear designer and fashion writer Alan Flusser, who is famous for providing the suits for Michael Douglas's most iconic on-screen character, the unethical financier Gordon ("Greed is good") Gekko in the film *Wall Street*. Flusser had this to say about the novice suit wearer's most basic demand: "There's a different mentality between a man and a woman [when it comes to fashion]. A woman dresses to attract. A man dresses to a certain degree to fit in. If a woman goes to a function and another woman is wearing the same dress as she, it's a disaster. If a man goes to a party and he's wearing a blue suit and everyone else is wearing a blue suit, he feels pretty comfortable." My suit was a disaster. At a moment when I needed to fit in, it made me feel conspicuous. I felt a deep shame. I had been betrayed.

As graduation drew closer, I started to imagine the kind of suits my classmates would wear. I could see them at convocation walking across the quad at Green College dressed in a Hugo Boss or a decent Calvin Klein looking ready to take on the future. They were at ease. They wore the mantle of a professional naturally. They were princes.

Graduation day came. Instead of going to my convocation, I went with Melissa and a good friend to celebrate at Hy's Steakhouse. In the dark wood–panelled, clubby cavern of Hy's, we toasted the memory of my father, who had died a few months earlier. Between the main course and dessert, I found myself appraising the room with his restaurateur's savvy. My steak came on a plank, and the wooden steak knife handle was well-worn – an authentic touch. The rare was medium. My father would have sent it back, but I didn't complain. His behaviour in restaurants used to embarrass me. In the name of research, he would steal menus, drink lists, cutlery, and napkins from other restaurants if he found them pleasing to the eye or to touch. If a waiter made an error, my father would quickly correct him. If a whole fish was being served, he would forbid the waiter to touch it. My father would stand up, usher him aside, and expertly handle the serving fork and spoon in one hand.

I was surprised by how much I missed him. The years of embarrassment, shame, anger, and struggle were over. Now, there was only a void. That's when I formulated a plan. My graduation present to myself would be a new, made-to-measure, custom-detailed suit.

A friend and colleague, Terry Donnelly, told me about an old, rundown shop on the corner of Carrall and Pender, the gateway to the city's historic Chinese district, and the intersection where Chinatown and Downtown meet. Modernize Tailors. He told me they had been there forever and they made good cheap suits. I should give them a try.

In the rain and cold of a December day I made my way to the shop. When I opened the door, an electronic bell went off. A short, elderly Chinese man appeared from behind a curtain-wall of unfinished jackets hanging from a pipe on the ceiling. He shuffled toward me.

"Hello, how can I help you?" It was Bill Wong.

I wasn't really sure. I asked him if I could look around the shop. He said sure and disappeared behind the jackets. The shop is a long tunnel of hundreds of bolts stacked haphazardly along the walls and on counters that run down the middle. I gravitated to a stack of flannels near the wall of coats. Bill poked his head through and asked, "What do you have in mind?"

I should have said, "The meaning of life." Instead, I said, "I'd like to order a suit."

"Okay," he said, straightening up.

He pulled me in front of a large armoire with three large mirrors and started to measure my chest, my stomach, my seat.

As he stretched the tape to size me up, I talked about Cary Grant. I told Bill I liked the way Grant looked in his films, in Indiscreet and Notorious, and that any man who could win the love of Ingrid Bergman was the role model for me. I wasn't sure about the suit's colour because the films were in black and white. Bill stopped me there.

"Anything that you like will look good on you."

He pulled out a bolt from among the many lining the left wall – a flannel. It wasn't one of the flannels I had been touching. It wasn't black, which would have been too artsy. It wasn't blue. It had texture; it was matte, not shiny. It felt relaxed. It wasn't corporate, yet in a pinch it would work as a proper dark suit. Charcoal grey = Cary Grant.

"The nice thing about this is it has a white fleck to it. It hides lint much better. You get a two-tone effect and depth."

This was the beginning of my sartorial education. Here was a man talking about wool like it was a fine wine or a painting. He taught me a grey flannel wasn't just grey. A truly great grey captures the entire spectrum of colour in its thread the way an oyster-grey sky can. Grey could have space within it. I also learned about the magic of Donegal tweed from Ireland. Donegal is a coarse-looking fabric in an ostensibly neutral brown, tan, or even blue tone. Up close, however, it rewards greater scrutiny. Woven in is a myriad of colours, including oranges, blacks, sky-blues, and reds. I learned you can match anything with a good

[23]

Donegal jacket, and the same is true with a well-flecked charcoal grey.

We talked about shoulders. He told me the British cut is built up with more padding in the chest and shoulder, hale and manly, and has higher armholes and a narrow waist. The Italian profile has the softness of a shirt shoulder but it can also sport roping: the sleeves cap, as if a loop of rope were stitched into the shoulders, with a mild pagoda–ski-jump flick upwards. The effect is Bowie-esque. I settled on an American or sack cut, which is soft-shouldered with a natural relaxed silhouette. As a point of reference, I had brought in a blazer I liked to wear – a dark, half-lined vintage piece I found at the Deluxe Junk Company in Vancouver.

"Ah, the Ivy League cut. See, it has a straight drop. No waist suppression. It has a hooked vent. Do you want a hooked vent?"

Ivy League, straight drop, waist suppression, hooked vent – the words were intoxicating. What was a hooked vent?

Bill pointed at the vertical seam along the back of the jacket. Instead of running straight down to the jacket hem, the seam took a radical right turn to indicate where the back slit began.

"I haven't seen this in fifty years," he said.

Bill inspected the blazer, pulling at the thread and turning it over. *Hooked vent.* He kept saying the words over and over again, patting the jacket like it was a cat. I really think it was the hooked vent that cemented our friendship.

"Now, how tall are you?"

"I'm five-foot-six. Actually, I'm five-five and three-quarters. I thought you should know because I don't want to throw you off."

Bill looked at me. I was being an idiot but he just laughed. He asked me to put on the Ivy League so he could measure me again, this time to see how loose the coat was on me. I told him about my father and how he had died a few months earlier. It was a pretty serious conversation to have with a stranger, but tailors, I would discover, are like bartenders and barbers: they are able to create spheres of intimacy in public places.

He straightened up and dusted off his pants. "You dress left."

I looked down. Bill patted between my legs. Extra fabric would have to be added at the left crotch point. "Yeah, you dress left."

This is when I discovered how difficult it is to back out of a commitment to purchase. Once a tailor touches your crotch, you are all in. Be prepared to put up a sizable deposit or payment in full. We agreed he would make me a three-button flannel (in the winter of 2001, the two-button jacket had yet to make its fashion comeback) with narrow lapels and a hooked vent. It would be tight at the shoulders and tight around the body, but it would fall straight down rather than have an hourglass shape. My own muscles would give the suit definition. But, but, but . . . Bill worked me out the door and onto the sidewalk.

I immediately felt buyer's remorse. I started to worry. Had we picked the wrong shade of grey? Would I walk into the light of day and realize it looked terrible in sunlight? What if it made my skin look sallow? What if it made me feel like I was wearing one of my father's suits? What could I say? Bill was my tailor. Isn't that the same as saying he is my doctor, my closing pitcher, my guy? If I didn't trust him on the matter of the suit, whom could I trust? And yet for the next two weeks, I was absolutely, positively sure we had picked the wrong shade of grey.

When I returned to the shop, Bill put me in front of the trifold mirror in my Ivy League suit with a straight drop, no waist suppression, and hooked vent.

Now I saw these weren't just words. What I saw in the mirror were ideas, ideas that had shapes. And these shapes could fill the spaces in my heart. If the shoulders of my spirit drooped, or I felt I could not hold my head high, this suit would straighten my back.

There was no other suit like it in the world. There was no weight. No history. No story yet. Just me.

I HAVE TO MAKE A CONFESSION. MY FATHER'S SUIT, compared with the suits he owned in the past, doesn't deserve the time and effort I am going to put into it.

A sensible tailor would tell me to buy a new suit that fits me and save myself the trouble. I understand it makes for a poor family heirloom, that it is ordinary, that it isn't so different from the odd-fitting, hand-me-down suits you will find in many closets.

Even an apprentice tailor could tell you that no ancient, nearsighted Italian whose middle finger has turned into a giant callus because he stopped using a thimble forty years ago was involved in hand-stitching it by gaslight. No one carved the buttons out of the horn of a near-extinct creature that once grazed on the grasslands of Africa. The buttons are dull brass. There is no silk twist, the all-important thread hoarded by Simpkin the Cat in Beatrix Potter's children's story "The Tailor of Gloucester." The thread on my father's suit is probably industrial polycotton, sold by the tens of thousands of metres and applied by machine on a production line. The suit is without distinction.

The quality of my father's clothes, in retrospect, makes for a good barometer of our family fortunes. In 1973 when, at the age of twenty-four, he was promoted to day manager of the glamorous Kon-Tiki Polynesian Restaurant and anointed an up-and-comer by the lounge's owner, his clothes were already impeccable.

The one photo I have of him from that time comes from my Uncle Jim. It's a black-and-white eight-by-ten of my father sitting on a wicker chair with a large oval back. The Polynesian decor suggests it was taken while he was on the job at the lounge. I remember the Kon-Tiki had two mammoth Easter Island–styled carvings at the entrance, a fake volcano surrounded by a glowing red fountain, and walls covered with bamboo strips. If I were to guess, I'd say the suit my father is wearing is a grey or royal blue wool. Simple, yet its lighter tone suggests summer nights and sophistication. It is certainly an off-the-rack. The lapel stitches are overly long (I can count them), but not criminal. What is impressive is the fit of the shoulders, the fall along natural lines without turning his deltoids into ham hocks, one of the dangers of tight and unpadded shoulders. I don't think I've ever looked as young and fresh as he does here. Everything about him seems light and lithe. But there are hints of hardness. His jaw is square and cut. The veins in one of his hands pop out in the same way mine do when I work too hard and stay up too late. Still, he looks unbelievably young and happy. I wish there were more such photographs of him.

After he left the Kon-Tiki to start his own restaurants and

consulting businesses, my father's spending on clothes and everything else escalated. By then we had moved from a modest duplex in Montreal's Notre-Dame-de-Grâce district, where Jews, Jamaicans, Italians, and Chinese lived side by side with anglo bohemians, to an upper-middle-class suburb over the bridge called Saint-Lambert. The president of the Canadian National Railway lived across the street. A department store magnate lived behind the elementary school a few blocks up. A Montreal Canadiens defenceman, the aptly named Guy Lapointe, used to buy his milk at the corner store or, as we called it, the *dépanneur*. This is the period when my father's wardrobe became opulent. He would wear sky-blue sports jackets with white buttons. Many of his suits were made to measure, meaning a tailor would sew him a suit on order based on a standard design block that would be adjusted to fit my father's precise measurements. He also owned a few custom-made suits, for which his tailor created a pattern specifically for my father by taking his measures and inputting them into a formula that generated a unique pattern on thick brown cardboard called oak-tag.

My father knotted his large patterned ties thick. He sported aviator sunglasses that hinted at his aspirations for a jet-setting life. Bold cufflinks became part of his repertoire. There's no other way to put it: my father started living – and looking – like a big shot.

Then my father's projects foundered. He went into a long decline, and so did the quality of his clothes.

This suit is an artefact of one of the bad times, long after he finally divorced my mother, after he stuffed what he could into a blue Ford Escort (many steps down from simultaneously owning a Buick Park Avenue, a Volkswagen Jetta, and an Oldsmobile Delta 88 Holiday Sedan) and crossed the country to live in Vancouver, where he was reduced to selling encyclopedias door-to-door. This is the backstory of my father's suit.

It now sags in a bad way, the way I imagine Willy Loman's suit sagged in *Death of a Salesman*. Like a balloon once filled with buoyant air and then deflated. The balloon doesn't return to its original state. Instead, the surface is stretched and, once empty, deformed with wrinkles. It is an ugly, exhausted thing.

This suit was bought off the rack and may have cost no more than $300. Even less, if, as I suspect, it was purchased on deep discount. I believe a label once hung on the inside lining, which would have told you it came from Bridge and Tunnel Tailors, a national chain of menswear shops. In an inner-lining pocket, the union tag with a string of style and lot numbers suggests it may have come from B & T's Kut-Rite Factory in Toronto, which closed after production was shipped offshore to places like China, Turkey, and Romania. Frankly, the suit is cheap. Not quite Romanian cheap, but cheap nonetheless.

Cheapness, however, is not my problem with the suit. If you're lucky enough to have a body that is just the right shape, even a cheap, ready-made, off-the-rack suit might look nearly as good from a distance as a work of sartorial genius from Savile Row (more on that later). The price point doesn't matter if you look good in the suit.

No, the problem here is the style. The suit's most general

details – blue, single-breasted, notched lapel, double-pleated pants with wide legs and patch pockets – are acceptable. But the cut, the inflection, where it tries to get fancy are where the problems lie. It is a plain, conservative, working-stiff suit tricked out with details to try to make it look better than it is. It doesn't succeed.

The jacket mangles the laws of proportion and geometry in an effort to be fashionable and up to date, if up to date means partying like it's 1989. The suit dates hard the way the turquoise-and-black sports jersey colours for professional expansion teams like the San Jose Sharks, the Carolina Panthers, and the Memphis Grizzlies cannot shake their moments of creation in the 1990s. The suit is a walking expiry date.

Trained eyes will see how it strives to emulate early Giorgio Armani. It desperately wants to reach the louche, sexual swagger and athleticism of Milan's giant of menswear. A man in early Armani makes his pelvis the centre of attention. The concept is potency, fabric falling from the shoulders and draping down, continuing through the pants, which are full over thick, muscular thighs. But it is not so in my father's suit. Much had been lost in translation between the precision, construction, and craft of a true Armani and what was cooked up by a team of design hacks at Bridge and Tunnel. It is a shadow of what should have been.

IF YOU'VE WONDERED HOW A MAN CAN LOOK deadly, dangerous, knife-like (indeed, this is how I imagine myself) even in the simplest and most humble dark suit, consider the suit's ancestral origins. Deep in its fibrous DNA, the suit was built for war.

In the late Middle Ages, the first suits were born not of wool, or cotton, or linen. They were made of metal and leather and a small pinch of youthful rebellion. The first suits were suits of metal-plate armour. Because it was heavy and its performance demands even heavier, the costume required optimal lightness and protection. Pulling the plate tightly around the limbs and body reduced the amount of material required. A tighter fit made the armour lighter. Still, it was best worn by the young and the fit. It also suited the adventurous, the hopelessly romantic, someone prone to inflict violence and willing to receive it. In other words, a knight.

Before the first suit, knights essentially wore giant chemises of chain mail called hauberks. As they began to experiment with sheets of metal in search of greater protection, their armourers initially created suits that followed the lines of hauberks: long, modest, leg-covering tunics of steel. But the knights soon discovered that a long surcoat (that's the part that covers the torso) interfered with leg movement. Shortening the surcoat gave the knights more freedom of movement. The suit put modesty aside for the most practical of reasons – to keep the wearer alive. As a result, some of its details were revealing. In writing about a fourteenth-century depiction of Edward, the Prince of Wales, aka the Black Prince, in which the prince wears a surcoat belted at the waist (forming a skirt that in modern parlance would be described as a mini), fashion historian Diana de Marly notes, "Its dagged hemline is of a shortness that shocked the moralists, and the ornate belt drew eyes to the sexual region in flagrant masculine display."

One could forgive the affront. It wouldn't do to have a sword pommel caught in a surcoat skirt or to have a knight stumble because a hem was lengthened for modesty's sake. Knights were the ones who did the fighting and the dying, as young men still do now, and they refused to compromise on protection and manoeuvrability during battle because they were showing too much leg.

No one could deny the new suit was becoming. In the era of muscular kinetic warfare, when bashing and slashing were vital ingredients for victory on the field of battle, all warriors shared the same attractive physical traits and winning form: powerfully built but lanky arms, broad shoulders atop a waspish torso and waist, and long, powerful legs. As military historian John Keegan writes about the young world-conquering Alexander the Great, the shape of the hero projected "an urgent, impatient boyishness, which was to determine the style in which heroes would be depicted in Western art from his day to ours."

This "urgent, impatient boyishness" soon found sartorial expression off the battlefield. Young knights began to wear short tunics and tight hosiery that revealed their legs, pelvis, and the outline of their genitals. Then there were cotes and doublets. These form-fitting coats took inspiration from plate armour while introducing buttons to the front of the suit, making it easier for men to put on tops without having to negotiate a neck hole. The cote became all the rage, and as de Marly explains in *Fashion for Men: An Illustrated History*, it gave rise to the art of tailoring as we know it: "Any peasant family could make their own simple tunics, for little cutting and fitting was necessary, but cotes had to be tailored by experts." And tailored they were. Cotes could be made tight at the waist, which emphasized what tailors now call "the drop": the difference in measure between the chest and the waist. Knights with heroic figures had found the perfect garment to show off their bellipotent physiques. Where a knight could not match the heroic proportions of Alexander, tailors made themselves busy by devising ingenious ways to pad the cotes in all the right places. From the very beginning, the suit found itself caught between the naked truth of the body and the elusive search for an ideal.

As the appetite for form-fitting tops caught on and the geometric complexity of the upper body became clear, so came the innovations of buttons and a better pattern. To work around the angles of the torso, tailors began to emulate the tectonic logic of plate armour by using darts and seams to pull fabric tightly around the male body. A doublet could require eight or more plates or panels to achieve the perfect fit.

They caused a scandal.

In *The Canterbury Tales*, Chaucer makes the complaint clear through his Parson: "Alas! Some of them show the very boss of the penis and the horrible pushed-out testicles that look like the malady of hernia in the wrapping of their hose, and the buttocks of such persons look like the hinder parts of a she-ape in the full of the moon . . . in that part of their body where they purge their stinking ordure, that foul part show they to the people proudly in despite of decency."

After millennia of being hidden beneath wraps, tunics, caftans, robes, and skirts – all garments now more associated with female dress – men's bodies were being shown off.

And so it began, the suit's path to hell.

FOR MOST OF MY CHILDHOOD, MY FATHER ALWAYS
had to work late. It was part of working in the restaurant
business. By the time we moved to Saint-Lambert from
Notre-Dame-de-Grâce in the spring of 1977, our family had
developed a routine. My mum served the children dinner at
five in the afternoon. We watched television and went to bed
at around nine. Eventually, my father returned home. On
certain nights, my mother would rouse all the kids out of
bed so we could sit with him. Tammy, who was older than
me by eleven months and the insomniac, would never be
groggy. Aimee, three years younger than me, would hardly
be awake. Lenny, who was still a baby, stayed asleep in bed.

In the kitchen, we would find my father sitting at the big
yellow kitchen table with brown paper bags opened to
reveal smoked meat sandwiches from Ben's Delicatessen.
They would be wrapped in aluminum foil. Pickles were
found shoved into sleeves of crinkled wax paper. Sometimes
I would not get out of bed right away but wait for the sound

of the brown paper bags being ripped open. As I entered the kitchen, the smell of brine would hit my nose.

We would sit together and have a second supper with him.

I loved the way he took off his jacket and loosened his tie and rolled up his sleeves. His forearms were meaty and pale. His face was always oily. He would wipe his glasses and tell us stories about the people he had met at the Kon-Tiki.

"I met the Platters today," he'd say, or "I met Trini Lopez once."

"Who's he?"

"He sings the 'Lemon Tree' song." To demonstrate, my father sinks into a false baritone. I find his crooning, serious and tuneful, embarrassing. The lyrics, a warning against sweet-looking but bitter-tasting fruit, make no sense to me.

On rare, special Saturdays, the traditional day off for general managers but not A-team restaurant staff, I would tag along with my father on his pre-lunch rounds of downtown Montreal. He and I would have backstage access to the bistros, steak houses, and drinking holes along Saint Catherine Street. We would visit before opening, when the kitchens were full and busy with prep work. He would visit alumni from his days at Ruby Foo's, who had worked with him as a waiter or busboy. By then they were all floor managers or executive chefs. It was like they were a band of pirates with matching tattoos. The bonds they shared couldn't be broken. Sometimes he would even bring me to the Kon-Tiki. I used to think it was because he had unfinished business at the shop, but I realize now he was taking the opportunity to show off his eldest son to the crew who knew him best.

I used to help take out the empty bottles and stack them in a storage area. Once in a while I had the job of loading full juice and beer bottles into the coolers under the bar. My reward would be Jell-O or ice cream mountains piled into mixing bowls or on cake platters. Later in the afternoon, he would take me past the strip bars on Saint Laurent Boulevard and into the Montreal Pool Room, where they served steamed hot dogs piled with onions and fries stuffed into greasy craft paper bags.

We would eat outside on the sidewalk. Actually, I would eat on the sidewalk. My father, still in his twenties, would lean against the nicest car he could find – somebody else's Continental, Chevy SS, or Italian coupe. I always felt he was daring the world to knock him off his perch. No one did. I have no clue what my father was trying to prove, but even then I knew it had something to do with being a man. I remember the tight-cut Glen plaid sports coat with blue checks he would wear with Bermuda blue pants, not as light as sky blue, not as dark as royal. His Bally shoes – and only Bally always. And the way he would pop his hands out of his sleeves to get them clear of the jacket and cufflinks so he could take the first bite with gusto.

THE FIRST CHANGE I'LL MAKE TO MY FATHER'S SUIT will be to the lapels. In my mind, lapels always come first; before shoulder width, the number of buttons, even colour.

Lapels are where the eyes fall. With their width and the quality of how they unfold, turning the facing wool from the inside out, they set the tone and the theme; they provide the overture for the suit. Most people focus on whether the lapels are peaked (the lapels point upwards like the alert ears of a cat) or the more common notched (these look as if a short-beaked bird has taken a bite out of the lapels near the clavicle). While interesting and certainly a function of fashion (each rises and falls in popularity), peaks and notches are not important to the success of a suit. What is important is the proportion and the manner in which they sit on the chest. The relevant question is, "Are your lapels sexy?"

Admittedly, *lapel* isn't a sexy word, but as the part of the jacket front that flips open to expose the shirt and, more

importantly, the throat and chest, lapels are positively erotic. They are the suggestive soft part of the suit.

The French call the point where the lapel and collar meet the *gorge* (throat). A lovely word used by the English as well, the gorge suggests mystery, depth, and danger. One could fall into it and never come back up.

Originally, there was no lapel on the coat. A man either wore his coat open or buttoned up over his sternum and up to his neck, which would be dressed with a ruff, a lace collar, or a cravat. Then it dawned upon some young men to leave the top buttons open. This practice of artful dishevelment seemed to amplify the dashingness of a suit: it gave the wearer a romantic windswept look, as if his clothes had been just slightly undone by vigorous horse riding. It became formalized when the front flaps of the coat were permanently folded out.

PEAKED LAPELS. ALTHOUGH *LAPEL* ISN'T A SEXY WORD, LAPELS ARE THE SUGGESTIVE SOFT PART OF THE SUIT.

Some assert a suit can't really be a suit without a lapel. Anne Hollander, in her authoritative study *Sex and Suits*, makes the argument that the suit really comes into being when tailors master the lapel and collar sometime between 1750 and 1800: "Its collar was forced by clever cut, steaming and stiffening to curve up and around the neck, to fold over and open out in front, and to form lapels that would obediently lie down and align themselves smoothly with the body of the coat. This perfectly tailored collar and flat-lying lapel still forms the most distinctive element of the modern suit-coat, and became the formal sign of modernity in dress."

Hollander's diction, with its tone of sado-masochism, says it all. You can almost hear the repeated crack and slackening of the whip with her use of the words *stiffening, curve,* and *obediently.* Why would a designer denude a garment of these wild energies?

NOTCHED LAPELS. AS THE PART OF THE JACKET THAT FLIPS OPEN TO EXPOSE THE SHIRT, THROAT, AND CHEST, LAPELS ARE POSITIVELY EROTIC.

Note, though, I am wrong to say a lapel is "folded." With a fold one thinks of a harsh line or edge as on a wing of a paper airplane. True tailors actually call the turning of the lapel from the inside out the "roll." Done properly the lapel will not look folded out at all. Instead it will roll out like a blooming flower petal. A great lapel should remind one of the bee-stung lips of Angelina Jolie, all fullness and sensuality. They are wool labia opening out with an irresistible lushness. With great lapels, the most masculine article in the man's arsenal, the suit comes alive with a feminine opening, which perhaps explains the enduring phallic nature of the essential suit accessory: the long tie.

Lapels can be – should be – kinky, dangerous, sleek, potent. To wit: if someone touches your suit sleeve, you're onto something good; if he or she strokes your lapel, the deal has been sealed. Hail a taxi and have at thee. All men deserve beautifully rolled lapels.

Of course, from time to time, there have been attempts to challenge the indispensability of lapels, but suits look odd without them. Both London dressmaker Sir Hardy Amies and the French designer Pierre Cardin tried to introduce lapel-less versions in the 1960s.

Amies first came to prominence during the Second World War when the couture houses of Paris were cut off by the occupation and London became for a short time the fashion capital of the world. By 1951 he started making dresses for the Queen. In 1964 he wrote *ABC of Men's Fashion* – "A man should look as if he has bought his clothes with intelligence, put them on with care, and then forgotten all about them" – and it was around this time that he made his great contribution to menswear: the ghillie-collared suit. The ghillie (not to be confused with the camouflage ghillie suit worn by hunters and snipers) had a shirt-styled collar and was buttoned up the front and to the neck and therefore lapel-less. It was a signature flourish for the designer but, to Amies's regret, it never quite caught on.

Pierre Cardin's own attempt removed both the lapel and the collar from the formula. Introduced in 1960, the Cylinder (aka Youth) line jacket featured five buttons up to the neck. Its look straddled monkish asceticism and a scientist's lab coat. It tells the story of the vertical without distraction and heralded Cardin as a truly modern designer, pushing clothes towards pure geometric blocks of colour and extreme minimalism, but in a historical context it was a devolution of form. Regardless, his perceived avant-gardism caught on. Three years later the Beatles adopted a similar look to replace the leather rocker jackets they wore while in Hamburg. Their suits, also buttoned right to the tie knot, were made by Dougie Millings and were more popular than Cardin's design. In fact, this Beatles suit can still be ordered online. Before pulling out a credit card, one should take heed: the suit still suffers from poor proportions. Then as now, the round-neck suit has only three mother-of-pearl buttons to close the front. The fasteners, spaced too far apart, seem to float in a sea of grey, unable to bring coherence to the front of the suit.

But by the time the Beatles debuted on the *Ed Sullivan Show* in February 1964, the collarless jackets were gone. Millings instead created dark, sharp-fitting suits with collars and lapels. In comparison with Millings's collarless confection, the suits the Beatles wore for their American debut created strong diagonals with lapels, contrast collars, and narrow ties, which helped visually separate the shirt collars. The suits served the same purpose as the Sullivan stage set composed of giant arrows and radiating lines. They provided dynamism and sexual energy. The set drew the eye to the Beatles, and the Beatles' suits drew the eye to their faces. The Beatles had arrived. With lapels. The girls went wild.

It should be stressed that not all lapels are created equal. Simply having a lapel isn't a sartorial key to the sexual promised land. Moreover lapels shouldn't be reduced to a libidic principle. They are capable of expressing other ideas. Consider the width of the lapel. A pair of wides (lapels wider than three and a half inches) can suggest the wearer is an Italian plutocrat. A set of wides, especially if they are peaked, can also evoke flight and all things avian.

At the other end of the spectrum, a set of skinnies (lapels under three inches) were famously featured on a giant jacket, known as the Big Suit, worn by David Byrne during the Talking Heads' "Speaking in Tongues" tour in 1984, as documented in Jonathan Demme's concert film, *Stop Making Sense*. Those lapels arrived at a cultural moment when the gay rights movement had emerged but the full impact of AIDS had yet to be felt or understood; when masculine identity had shifted away from the rock-solid archetypes of the old-school masculinities of Sinatra, McQueen, Eastwood, Wayne. Other possible male identities were being lofted on FM radio, where androgynous singers ruled the charts: Prince, Adam Ant, Morrissey, the Pet Shop Boys, George Michael, the guy from a-ha, and Boy George. Girls and boys could love them equally. Then there was Byrne, nerdy, energetic, surreal, and ironic, with his tiny lapels suspended between outrageously oversized shoulder pads. They suggested the ridiculousness and impotence of inflated machismo and spoke to a generation brought up on New Wave who viewed the man in the power suit with suspicion. They struck a chord, proportional laws be damned. (A year after its theatrical release, midnight screenings of *Stop Making Sense* started to pop up across North America, and men and women started attending in their Big Suits. Prizes were given out for the best of the night.)

Returning to the wide side, the ultra-wide lapels of the zoot suit of the late 1930s and 1940s could exceed five inches. Most people know the look: long, draping suit jackets with extra-wide pleated pants narrowing or pegged with turn-up pant cuffs. Some say it was inspired by the civilian dress of the British Guardsmen, who all wore broad-shouldered, full-skirted suits when off duty. Another zoot suit origin story posits a busboy in Gainesville, Georgia, created the zoot suit when he tried to dress like Rhett Butler. There may have been a parallel development of the style, but what is certain is the zoot suit's exaggerated lines and gaudy proportions caught the eye of gangsters and jazz performers, people not prone to conservative fashion choices.

In their overview of male fashion archetypes, *Jocks and Nerds*, Richard Martin and Harold Koda describe the zoot suit's appeal this way: "It represents an ideal of adolescent rebellion: to enjoy the time of adulthood without its restraints, to live in an era of style exaggeration before all becomes sublimated and suborned."

One such rebel was a fifteen-year-old named Malcolm Little. He later described his 1941 experience of buying his first zoot suit in his eponymous autobiography, *Malcolm X*:

I was measured, and the young salesman picked off a rack a zoot suit that was just wild: sky-blue pants thirty inches in the knee and angle narrowed down to twelve inches at the bottom, and a long coat that pinched my waist and flared out below my knees. . . . I took three of those twenty-five cent sepia-toned, while-you-wait pictures of myself, posed the way "hipsters" wearing their zoots would "cool it" — hat angled, knees drawn close together, feet wide apart, both index fingers jabbed toward the floor. The long coat and swinging chain and the Punjab pants were much more dramatic if you stood that way.

Zoot suits also became popular among the Pachucos, a subculture of alienated Mexican-American youth living in Texas, Arizona, and California. In Los Angeles during the Second World War, the Pachucos had become an affront to the mainstream. At the time wool was a restricted material, dedicated to making uniforms. Bomber crews wore shearling for warmth. The lanolin from wool could be used for gun oil. To reduce civilian consumption, suitmakers were restricted from using more wool than was necessary. Producing double-breasted suits or turn-up pant cuffs were considered unpatriotic acts. Wide legs and pleats were simply treasonous. Some tailors ignored the ban, went underground, and continued to furnish the style to young Latinos who found themselves flush with cash. After years of racism and limited opportunities, the Pachucos had finally gained access to employment in heavy industries supporting the war effort.

Of course, this irony was lost to the sailors on shore leave who cabbed into East L.A. looking for a fight. What was really happening was anti-Latino racism had hitched a ride on the bandwagon of patriotism. Fights escalated throughout the summer of 1943. The servicemen would beat the teens, strip them of their clothes even if they weren't wearing zoot suits, and shave off their hair. Eventually the conflict spread to other parts of the city, including the black neighbourhood of Watts, and a full-scale, nationwide panic erupted. Editorials appeared in the New York Times and Los Angeles Times. Life magazine published a photo-exposé on the sordid world of the zooties. First Lady Eleanor Roosevelt defended the Mexican zooties in the press. The whole affair became known as the Zoot Suit Riots and, while matters of socioeconomic disparity and racism were at the heart of the crisis, no one can deny the role played by an extra inch or two of wool.

☿

Exactly how much lapel is too much lapel on my father's suit?

They measure four inches. They are to my reckoning too wide. But how much to take away eludes me. I suppose I could very easily slice off an inch and make it conform to the current standard of three-inch lapels. But then I would just be falling into line. Another sheep in serge clothing. Whatever dimension I settle on, it should be one based on who I am, my desires, the image I wish to project.

In the past, holy geometries have risen out of the body. Men like Michelangelo and Leonardo carved up cadavers to discover the secret harmony of the body. There are equations into which I can plug my measurements and ostensibly derive the best width for a lapel. The idea of following someone else's law makes me reluctant.

Either way, it isn't easy to cleave into a whole and sound garment with a pair of shears. It goes against any natural instinct. It is an act of annihilation. It is the opening of Pandora's box and a call for high-order mayhem. Lopping off two or more inches of wool can sometimes feel like diving off a cliff with the hope the water below is deep enough so you don't go splat but not so deep you'll drown. You have to lie to yourself just a bit. You have to tell yourself it's going to be all right.

Except I have no clue how to do this. As a guide I have *Classic Tailoring Techniques: A Construction Guide for Men's Wear* by Roberto Cabrera and Patricia Flaherty Meyers. The manual provides step-by-step instructions on how to build a suit from scratch. It says, "Wide lapels and pleated trousers may combine to create too heavy an impression for a shorter man, slightly built. . . . None of this is gospel. Use your eye and trust your judgment."

Okay, not exactly what the doctor ordered. Maybe I will have to fall back on traditional edicts. In front of the mirror with the jacket on, I decide I can't leave it be at four inches. I measure a less than manly thirty-eight inches at the chest. Viewed from the front, in my father's suit I present a breadth of only sixteen inches. Half my chest is taken up with his lapels.

Not a good thing. In tailoring, as in most other visual arts, we try for proportions that avoid dividing the body in half. Details that introduce asymmetry are a good thing (consider the sole breast pocket). Suit elements need to be slightly off to the side, instead of dead centre, to make the whole composition more dynamic. A coat hem that divides the upper and lower body in half is a tragedy; it makes for a deadening, unflattering proportion. Shifting it a few inches can make a torso appear neat and trim and give the illusion of longer legs. Admittedly a delicate adjustment, one to do by eye rather than by measuring tape, but should I?

I baste a line of stitches along the lapels making them no wider than one-third my chest size when viewed from the front. I baste a dash-dash-dash line of contrast-coloured thread over the navy, using a heavy orange thread from a giant 10,000-yard spool.

The best part about baste stitching is that it is sewing without commitment. No fabric is damaged. It is the secret tool of haute couture and tailoring. Baste a thousand times. Cut and sew only once. It reminds me of sketching, or underpainting, or the way I used to draft floor plans with a 9H pencil, a lead as hard as a nail. There was no commitment.

My problem is I can't stop basting. Instead of plowing along, one-third lapels, full speed ahead, I start basting alternate cutlines. How about at the three-tenths mark? Wouldn't that be more refined and subtle? I mean, the law of thirds is so obvious. I put down one track of baste stitches after another. Soon the jacket starts to look like a map of the London Underground. I have become lost. Yet the more I handle the suit the more I remember about my father.

My fondest memories are of wrestling with him on weekends. My fighting style was a synthesis of Batroc the Leaper (Captain America's nemesis), the giant robot karate moves of Ultraman, and the ancient techniques taught at the Shatner

School of Hand-to-Hand Combat for Starfleet Officers. We would clear space in the living room and I would unleash a series of double-fisted blows on my father's back until he collapsed on the ground. But it was always a ruse. I would jump on him and that was my fatal error because he was an expert grappler. Gently but firmly, he would begin to use Greco-Roman locks to twist me into a pretzel. My father would fold and refold me until I was a small ball and then pin me in such a way that my back was to the floor and every other part of me, it seemed, was trapped under the dome of his body. I saw only darkness and, through a crack of light between his forearms, a portion of his face, big, round, moonlike. He was the sky and the horizon and I was never happier as a child than when I was enveloped by his warm, comforting presence.

A man's first duty is to his tailor.

Oscar Wilde

I IMAGINE YOU MAY BE WONDERING AT THIS POINT, especially if you've ever followed a Burda or Vogue or McCall's pattern, or were forced to make a sweatshirt in home economics, if I am really up to the job of altering my father's suit – even if I am an apprentice. Sewing garments is hard and requires a certain temperament, but coatmaking is an even more exclusive arena of clothesmaking. In my opinion, it is the summit of all arts involving a needle and thread. Great coatmaking doesn't happen with a computer and a laser cutter. It doesn't take place in a factory in Shenzhen, China. It takes place in a tailor shop.

In the shop, working the front, is a tailor known as the cutter. Because of the intimacy required to do the job, the cutter will almost always be a man. He will measure the customer and offer nuggets of sartorial knowledge that will stay with the suit shopper for the rest of his life. If a cutter lays down a law like "This blue will always look better, more rich, more elegant with brown shoes," the pupil will never again be able to bring himself to lace on a pair of black Dack's or Church's oxfords with that particular shade of blue. If the cutter tells a shorter gentleman that shortening his coat sleeves to reveal a half-inch of shirt cuff – not a quarter- but a half-inch (perhaps tailors are engineers after all) – will do wonders in providing the illusion of greater length, only the very strong-willed will be able to resist the urge to alter the sleeves on all his suits. The cutter is the man you call "my tailor." He measures you. He pins you up. He takes all the notes for the special little details you have to have. He is the one who chats you up whilst you are peeling off your pants. He is the one you see walking around the shop carrying two-foot-long scissors.

This is all very impressive, but it is the coatmaker who really swings the big brass ones in the workshop. The coatmaker does the sewing. He is the one who works over every inch of your coat – and just the coat, the pants may go elsewhere to another tailor – with steam and probing fingertips and little tentative pricks of thread. He may even beat your suit-to-be with a hunk of wood called a clapper to give your garment the right shape, the internal life, the sheer finished perfection you thought only fictional characters like Bruce Wayne and James Bond could possess. Coatmaker: there is no tailor's shop without one, but the life isn't easy. Sometimes a price is exacted. In the nineteenth century, medical experts worried coatmakers were susceptible to work-related aneurysms. Eye strain and repetitive stress injuries are part of the job. Do ten thousand stitches per coat every two days, six days a week for forty-five years, and you may end up lonely, misanthropic, incapable of carrying on a conversation. Tailoring is not for everyone – but I think it might be for me.

I hope it is as I've been at loose ends. My dreams for a career as a hard-hitting journalist are dead in the water. I've developed a reputation for being light. I'm the guy who writes about fashion and design. The chances I will cover wars, politics, crime, and anonymous government leaks are nil. There are no Pulitzer Prizes or Peabodys awarded for exposés on the spring/summer collections. Which I accept. I still believe fashion matters. It matters to people not because they care what someone in Paris or New York has to say about what they should wear next season, nor because they think what models and Hollywood starlets wear is vital to their happiness. Fashion matters because every day people get up in the morning and, with the palette of clothes they find in their closets and dressers, they attempt to create a visual poem about a part of themselves they wish to share with the world. That's what fashion has always meant to me. Then there's the shop to consider.

Long after they made me my first made-to-measure suit, I found myself visiting Modernize Tailors and hanging out with Bill Wong and his younger brother, Jack; Park Wong, a cousin and the coatmaker; and Laddie, who makes the pants. I went there to be around Bill. Still do.

When I walk into the shop, a place filled with men beyond retirement age, I feel I am at home in a way I never felt in a newsroom or in a story meeting. I love being here. I like the way the day passes, the solace and peace. I am fascinated by how slowly, without anxiety, the tailors create jackets and pants. With them I can almost believe I've found my place in the world. I have arrived.

I think I must miss having older Chinese men in my life. My grandfathers are in Montreal, my father is dead. If I sometimes wonder what I'll be like in twenty or thirty years, I have only to look at Bill and I feel reassured.

Watching Bill work with the customers is a treat. He lavishes them with care and attention. I could never do that as a journalist. The customers respect him and take his advice with acceptance and gratitude. While the shop as a commercial venture has become borderline, Bill has a loyal cadre of aging lawyers, judges, brokers, and real estate moguls marching in every few months to order a suit. I think they want his company as much as I do. He provides a bridge to a bygone era when all men wore suits in the city and there were supper clubs like the Cave and Isy's, which drew in acts like Ella Fitzgerald and Tony Bennett back in the 1950s and 1960s. Bill makes everyone feel like a million bucks. I watch him and I think that could be me.

I like the whole master-and-apprentice deal. I've had bosses. I've had editors. I was raised to address men and women of any age as Sir, Ma'am, or Miss, but to call someone your master is very Jedi Council. Bill deserves the title. Though his hands are gnarled with arthritis and the intelligent eyes set in his broad face show signs of cataracts, he can do the work. Don't let the Coke-bottle lenses in his glasses or the thin wispy white hairs on the top of his head fool you. He has a heavy, lobster claw–like thumbnail he uses to pick thread. His hands and fingertips can detect the smallest flaws in construction. They tell him when a seam is too thick or uneven. He may shuffle but he is spry. I also like his impish quality. It is nice to know an old man who likes to giggle. I like Bill being my master and I like learning to sew. I like how one can take all the scraps and stitch them together so they make sense, so that they make something whole. Every piece has its place. And maybe so does every moment in life, no matter how dark or sad.

When I asked Bill if he would let me be his apprentice, he tried to talk me out of it.

"What? You don't want to be an apprentice. No one wants to be a tailor anymore. What you should do is go to fashion school and become a designer."

He was right. One look around the shop is all the proof you need. The youngest tailor among them, the youthfully named "Laddie," is sixty-nine. And Bill is no spring chicken. His family wants him to retire. Taking on a thirty-seven-year-old apprentice isn't such a brilliant idea. A coatmaker requires four to seven years to be fully competent. The legendary Frederick Scholte of London, tailor to the Duke of Windsor between 1919 and 1959, wouldn't let a trainee touch a coat without ten years of apprenticeship experience. My apprenticeship would be a race against time. Bill could be ninety-five before I will be ready. I was already too late, but still I asked Bill if I could be his apprentice for just a year to see if I would work out. Then Park, who is a sweet man but won't suffer fools, made his view be known: "You sweep the floor first."

And I agreed. I sweep floors. I stack magazines in the dressing room. I vacuum. I sort dozens of bolts by quality, colour, and pattern. The worst job is cleaning the washroom. It is very hard for old men to bend down. It was rarely cleaned before I arrived. That first time, as I scrubbed the outside of the toilet bowl, I didn't think about how disgusting it was, or how this was beneath a person with a graduate degree in architecture; all I could think was that they needed me.

[55]

ONE LATE AFTERNOON IN THE SUMMER OF 1977, a woman called the police. She could not find her eight-year-old son. It had been hours since she had last seen him. Her family was new to the neighbourhood; her husband had been promoted at work and with the extra income they bought a house in the suburbs. She had called all the neighbours that she knew and spoke with all the children her son had befriended. No one had seen him since lunch time. The police told her not to worry. They instructed her to call back if the boy had not returned by dusk. She couldn't wait. She instructed her eldest daughter to organize a search party. The girls mounted their bicycles and fanned out in pairs to patrol beyond the border streets and neighbourhoods he was forbidden to enter. The kid posse rode out past the elementary school six blocks away and picked their way through the wooded lot between the highway and an arterial boulevard beside the river, where the boy had started to build forts. The woman feared he would be found in the pond, drowned among the wet garbage, used condoms, and bulrushes.

For hours the children rang their bicycle bells and honked their horns, calling out the boy's name, but no answer came. The eldest daughter returned home with the bad news that he was still missing. Out of desperation, the woman decided to search every cupboard in the house. Perhaps he had accidentally poisoned himself. Perhaps he was playing a game of hide-and-seek that would earn him a hard spanking. She looked under the kitchen and bathroom sinks. She opened the long wall of cabinets in the basement where the family kept toys, sporting equipment, and old clothes. The boy would often climb into one of the cabinets with a flashlight and read comic books, but he was not there. Finally, she went through all the bedroom closets again. The last one she searched was in the master bedroom. Inside, she found him asleep. He had drawn the laundry over himself for warmth. He was naked except for three articles of clothing: crudely wrapped around his neck was a tie, half-pulled up his legs were a pair of black sheer nylons, and over his bare torso he had slipped on a blue double-breasted coat. I was that boy.

The next morning my father set me down at the foot of my bed.

"What does one need to live?"

"Food?"

"Wrong," he said. "You can spend $50 on food or $1,000. At the end of the month you will have nothing. If you spend $1,000 on how you dress, if you look good, clean, and presentable, you will never go hungry. Someone will always give you a chance to work for them. Then you can eat. Do you understand?"

I didn't.

He snapped a rolled-up tie in the air like a whip. Then he unfurled the tie, hung it over his arm, and lectured me on the difference between foulard and woven ties (the former have a printed pattern, the latter have a pattern created by weaving multi-coloured silk threads). My father went on to explain the value of a pair of calfskin Bally loafers. He urged me to touch the buttery brown hide. He made me hold them and I recall marvelling at how heavy they were. I told him so and he laughed. He pulled out the wooden trees and gave the shoes back to me. They were as light as they were soft. Then my father dressed me in one of his suits and cinched a belt around me so the pants stayed up. I clomped around in the loafers.

There would be other lessons: I would learn how to roll the sleeves of a dress shirt to the elbows in such a way that the edge of the cuff still showed and how to wear a belt with the buckle off to one side – more dashing than wearing it dead centre – but these came with less and less frequency. The lessons that followed would no longer be about clothes.

⌒

It had been a year full of change. My father was now general manager and the Kon-Tiki was his ship to captain. We had moved from our duplex in the urban residential district of Notre-Dame-de-Grâce to a bungalow in the South Shore suburb of Saint-Lambert. I had started grade three at a new school, where I met Paquito, who became my best and lifelong friend when we discovered we both went home to lunch instead of brown-bagging it in the basement cafeteria. From then on we did everything together: walked to and from school, played board games, climbed trees, read and drew comic books. He lived across the street and his bedroom window was opposite mine. We talked constantly about how we should draw a string across the road so we could speak to each other through tin cans from our beds. It never occurred to us to use the phone. With him, my life opened up beyond my family for the first time. A larger world came into existence.

Maybe that was why I didn't notice how my father had begun to change. This is when our family established its nocturnal routine. My father had always worked late, but now he no longer came home for a regular supper. Instead he came home at midnight. Then one a.m., then three a.m. There were nights he wouldn't come home at all. Inexplicably, to me at least, my father started to sleep in the car. This is when he started to drink heavily. At the time, I thought it was due to the pressures and demands of the restaurant business. I would discover decades later that my father had started seeing another woman. On those nights when I told myself he was working at the Kon-Tiki, he was actually taking out a woman named Mei Fong, who worked as a coat check girl at a Chinese restaurant. My mother's suspicions were confirmed when, after searching through his car, she found condoms in the glove compartment. She confronted him later that same night.

I didn't know it then but this was the point when our life together as a family started to unravel. It was not quick. It took a decade as, layer by layer, the illusions of domestic happiness were stripped away from the children, from me, with every fight and drunken outburst, and with every one of my father's car crashes. There were so many. He crashed coupes, sedans, foreign and domestic. As a boy, I assumed the frequent appearance of new cars in our driveway was a by-product of our new-found wealth and my father's need to flaunt it. In fact, the fleet of automobiles passing through our hands was due to a particular concrete median on the north end of the Victoria Bridge. When drunk, my father could never quite negotiate it. He always emerged unscathed, and it is a miracle he never hurt anyone else.

The beginning of the end came in my sleep. Through the thickness of sleep, I heard and felt things smashing and banging. Then I woke up. It was no nightmare. The noises were coming from down the hall.

I heard whimpering and crying that escalated to scream-ing. I thought a burglar had broken into our home. Someone was hurting my mother. I grabbed a pencil for a weapon and stuck my head out the door. The hall was dark but the lights were on in the kitchen.

I could see my mother in the full light. In silhouette, I saw my father picking up dishes and throwing them. They were striking the wall right next to my mother's head. The dishes were porcelain. I recall thinking how much they resembled snowballs on impact, spraying her with fine white shards as they exploded.

When he ran out of dishes, he started to throw pome-granates, my mother's favourite fruit. They left gory red stains and splatters of black seeds on the walls. When he had nothing left to throw, my father enveloped her in his arms.

It's going to be all right, I thought. He is just angry and now he is sorry. He'll never do it again. I stepped into the hallway, still clutching my pencil, inching closer to them. I was wrong.

My father began to squeeze and poke her hard to make some wordless point. My mother whimpered as he bruised her. I looked down at my pencil, then at my father. His shoulders were immense, full and round. I could see how heavily his arms hung down his sides and I felt shame. I knew there was nothing I could do.

Behind me, Aimee, three years old, opened her bedroom door. She rubbed her eyes. I backed up to her.

"Go back to sleep."

She pushed past me, oblivious to what was going on. She picked her way through the mess on the floor and grabbed my mother's hand.

"Mummy, come to bed," said Aimee.

My father loosened his grip and my mother slipped away from him. Then he stumbled past me and into the bathroom and fell asleep in the tub. Alone in the kitchen, I went to the counter and opened the utensil drawer. I pulled out a knife and took it to bed with me. It was for spreading butter.

When I woke up in the morning, my mother was gone.

My father spent the next few days with us, making breakfast, lunch, and dinner. We ate pancakes, French toast, and takeout pizza – he acted as if we were on vacation. When my sisters and I asked him where our mother had gone, he told us she was visiting our grandparents. We had to accept what he said as true. To do otherwise would be to surrender once again to the terror of that night. It was better to pretend his attentions, his attempts to step into our mother's place, were a prank that would end soon enough. Whether we believed him or not was beside the point. It was my first experience of powerlessness.

She returned three days later. There were no discussions, no explanations, no family meeting. My parents acted as if nothing had happened. Everything went back to normal, and as an eight-year-old you want nothing more than for things in your family to be normal. I said nothing. I did my best to forget. And, in fact, I did.

Only later would I learn from my mother that, after she had confronted him about his adultery, my father had told her he was leaving her for Mei, and he was leaving right away. Though late, my father had called Mei on the telephone in front of my mother to tell her the good news: they could be together.

It was Mei who stopped my father. She told him she didn't want to leave her husband. She told him to never call again. Then the line went dead in my father's hands. He was never the same man after that.

How can we expect that men should keep the command-
ments of God (I add, of the King) that preserve not the
lineaments of their bodies?

John Evelyn, "Tyrannus, or the Mode" (1661)

IN 1665, THE GREAT PLAGUE STRUCK ENGLAND,
killing eight thousand people a week in London. The total
number of deaths is estimated to be between seventy-five
thousand and one hundred thousand, 20 percent of the city's
population. A year later came the Great Fire, which consumed
London Bridge, destroyed thirteen thousand homes, and
cindered St. Paul's Cathedral. The diarist Samuel Pepys called
the inferno a "horrible, malicious flame," and observed confused pigeons hovering over their lost roosts. In his entry for
September 2, 1666, he recorded that the birds were "loth to
leave their houses, but hovered about the windows and bal-
conies till they were, some of them burned, their wings, and
fell down." The fire would rage for another two days.

Many believed the plague and fire were punishments sent
from God, and they thought the wayward behaviour of the
"Merry Monarch" King Charles II and his suite of courtiers,
the Merry Gang, was to blame. The young dukes, earls, and

baronets who gathered around the throne were notorious rakes and blades who drank, duelled, womanized, buggered, and caroused. In his judgment of a Merry Gang member, the lord chief justice may have been prescient when he declared "that it was for him, and such wicked wretches as he was, that God's anger and judgments hung over us."

Even the Merry Gang's clothes were an affront. They paraded about in a provocative, gender-defying manner that was "selfish, dissolute, effeminate." John Evelyn, an author, diarist, and appointee to several commissions by Charles II, watched in horror as men of the aristocracy became enamoured with ribbons, ruffles, lace, and high-heeled shoes (a fad imported from France). Coats, which had by then replaced the doublet, were made with long skirts. Underneath men wore bulging breeches called pantaloons. Breeches were meant to be knee-length pants, but in the mid-1600s they were cut so full in the thighs they ballooned skirt-like around the calves. The heroic form of the Middle Ages had given way to a bell shape, and the silhouettes of men now mimicked those of women. And then there was the makeup. Evelyn was so appalled that he published a pamphlet: "Behold we one of our Silken Camelions and aery Gallants making his addresses to his Mistress, and you would sometimes think yourself in the country of the Amazons, for it is not possible to say which is the more woman of the two coated Sardanapalus's."

Republicans, papists, Puritan writers, and the general public were certain the conflagration of London was the "dreadful fire of Sodom" and the earlier plague a divine judgment. When the ashes had barely cooled, a chastened

Charles II made a proclamation in council. He intended to impose a style of dress to appease the advocates of masculine restraint: men of the court would from then on wear a modest long vest of black cloth or velvet, edged with white satin, and over this waistcoat they would don an even longer black overcoat of the same material. Gone were the high-heeled shoes and stockings. Boots were now the footwear of choice. A week later, Charles appeared in a three-piece ensemble consisting of a vest "reaching the knee, having the sword girt over it, a loose coat, straight Spanish breeches ruffled with black ribbons, and buskins instead of shoes and stockings."

Courtiers fell into line but "there were those amongst his friends who offered him a wager he would not persist in wearing it long." They were right. Soon after, Charles II began to make modifications to his vest by removing the white piping. He claimed the contrasting white made him look like a magpie. By November, he had introduced a silk vest trimmed with silver. Following his example, the court responded by wearing jewelled vests made of cloth-of-silver. The final killing stroke to Charles II's reforms came in the form of a report from William Batelier, a French wig maker, who described how, in a brilliant act of knavery and psychological warfare, Louis XIV of France had begun dressing his servants according to Charles II's regulations. Contemporary historians will argue the report was wrong but the damage had been done. Charles II's determination withered. Within two years, men's fashion reverted back to its wanton ways. Ruffles continued to grow, feathers were capped, black curly periwigs became

longer (making the men look like seventeenth-century versions of Howard Stern). The contrite solemnity Charles II sought had evaporated.

But the idea of the vest endured and became a fixture in menswear and, in many ways, regained some of the propriety the Merry Monarch had attempted to enforce. Whether a fop or a Puritan, a gentleman would wear a vest or waistcoat under his jacket. And only the advent of central heating after the Second World War was able to weaken the hold of Charles II's lasting contribution to menswear – the three-piece suit.

CHARLES II INVENTED THE SOBER THREE-PIECE SUIT
TO AVOID DIVINE WRATH.

At Modernize Tailors, I should repeat here, we do mostly made-to-measure. Made-to-measure means we create suits for customers based on pattern blocks made of oak tag, a thick brown cardboard. For example, a pair of pants is based on two patterns: one for the front quarter and one for the back. For jackets, Modernize has sets of blocks for a thirty-six-inch chest up to a thunderous fifty-four-inch chest. These patterns hang on nails around the shop. When a suit is ordered, we use these patterns to create it. Of course, the cutter and the coatmaker will make adjustments to the pattern and the garment directly to make sure it fits the customer. But what we do should not be confused with bespoke tailoring.

Bespoke tailoring takes the idea of the perfect fit to another level. It involves a cutter creating a unique pattern specifically for the customer based on his measurements. It requires far more hand-stitching. The bespoke ideal is to bring the highest level of craft, finish, and quality to suits. It is the equivalent of haute couture for men. There is no place in the world that is more inextricably linked to the idea of "bespoke" than Savile Row in London, England.

Apart from the booming music emanating from a neighbouring Abercrombie & Fitch clothing shop (which, by the way, looks and feels like an amusement park funhouse upon entry), the most illustrious street in all of men's tailoring is (to a North American's eye) a narrow, quiet strip with small but luxurious storefronts. The first shop you will see is No. 1 Savile Row, the home of Gieves & Hawkes, who have been making bespoke suits for the last 240 years. They've made garments for a world-class clientele that spans politics and pop culture – and history – ranging from the Duke of Wellington and Winston Churchill to soccer player David Beckham.

A few more steps farther along is 10 Savile Row, the address of Dege & Skinner. While most bespoke firms have with time lost their direct connection to their founder (in 2007, Gieves & Hawkes lost cutter Robert Gieve, a fifth-generation descendant of one of the firm's co-founders), Dege & Skinner has William Skinner, the managing director of the company and the fourth generation of his family to run the business. (His father, Michael, is the firm's chairman.) Skinner has brown hair with three shocks of grey at the widow's peak and the sides. His face is reminiscent of a younger Alec Baldwin. He wears a striped blue club tie with a pink shirt and white contrasting collar. I recognize in him the classic personality of a front-of-shop man. He has an easygoing jocularity that makes him comfortable interacting with people from all walks of life. In his eyes, I can see how he watches people carefully in order to assess their unspoken needs. He also has an underlying firmness. Unless a custom tailor wants to find himself making clothes he despises, he has to be ready to say no from time to time. Skinner is such a man.

In the shop, along a frieze, over the bolts, bookcases, and armoires, is a line of photographs of what appear to be senior officers, royalty, and heads of state. Many are from Africa and the Middle East. Skinner notices I have a camera. He asks me not to include the photos in any shots I take of the shop.

I ask Skinner about the meaning of bespoke. In answer, he pulls out a tweed sports jacket. Inside, it is lined with a brilliant orange.

"This is a shooting suit," he says. "The reason I got this out is it has a special pleated back which was actually designed by my grandfather in the 1930s. It has a special construction, a lining that is elasticated, that gives you ease of movement to go and shoot. When you put the gun down, the pleats pull back into place. The look of the jacket remains smart."

The look, however, stands second to how bespoke feels. It is hard to understand how incredible wearing a bespoke suit can feel when most of us settle for ready-made clothes and simply tolerate the unavoidable flaws of fit. We hardly notice how our clothes rumple, pull, pinch, and generally disfigure our bodies or, more to the point, how the tugs of our clothes mangle our sense of self. The bespoke suit is created from direct knowledge of the wearer's body. His asymmetries, his posture, his disproportions are all taken into account. It is a satisfying and humanistic high art. To achieve it, the cutter delineates an individual pattern and hand-cuts out the fabric for a suit; the fabric is then handed over to a coatmaker and a trouser maker. Through a number of fittings or tryings-on, corrections are made. Seams will be sewn and ripped open again if necessary.

Skinner lets out a breath of air. "It can be time-consuming. But perfection doesn't happen automatically. It has to be strived to. You're dealing with a body or a shape that . . ." He pauses. "Let's just say, no two people are the same. Some people have figures that wouldn't fit into an off-the-rack, full stop."

The present conception of bespoke is an exacting process. Sewing machines are used but the majority of the work is still done by hand. Unlike a production-line suit, a current bespoke job calls for only one or two tailors to work on a coat. Often, a machine stitcher will be the only other person involved besides the coatmaker. The machine stitcher will sew ancillary components like the pockets and linings for all the other tailors, but once those parts are done he will pass the jacket back to the coatmaker, who will complete it with hand-stitches.

In 2008, the term *bespoke* was, in the minds of Skinner and the other Savile Row tailors, in danger of being corrupted. Online and discount made-to-measure companies, they said, were misusing the word. Specifically, they lodged a complaint with the Advertising Standards Association against Sartoriani London, a tailoring company founded in 2007. It has a store just around the block from Savile Row, another showroom in New York, and, ironically, an office-showroom in the same building as Dege & Skinner.

The Savile Row tailors argued Sartoriani London was misleading buyers by claiming their process was bespoke. In its defence, Sartoriani outlined their process. On a first appointment a customer selects from a range of fabrics and a book of styles. The customer then meets with a master tailor "who would take approximately 20 measurements and give guidance about the material and fit, if needed. . . . A length of cloth would then be cut and sent to their manufacturer in Germany along with the customer's measurements and specifications to be made up into a suit. The measurements and any individual requirements, such as style, buttons, sewing thread, tags, linings and any other items the customer may have specified, would be entered into the manufacturer's production computer."

Then the suit is sewn by machine and sent to the U.K. The customer tries it on. If alterations are needed, tailors make them in the showroom. The price: £495.

The advertising council focused on the meaning of the word *bespoke*. In the Savile Row tradition, bespoke refers to a bolt of cloth reserved for a particular customer. It is a pledge of quality. It means a tailor can't swap one bolt of fabric for another, even if it is the same colour, material, and texture. Even if it is sourced from the same mill and emerged from the same dye lot – it doesn't matter. Bespoke means, at its highest level, no sample book. A customer finds the 3.5 metres from which he wants a suit. A tailor writes with tailor's soap a set of initials or pins a note on the bolt. It is now "bespoken."

Unfortunately for the complainant, the ASA decided to refer to the dictionary. In the Oxford English Dictionary, bespoke is defined as, as the decision states, "made to order." The ASA ignored the fact that on Savile Row a suit has lapels and buttonholes that are hand-stitched. Linings are hand-felled with a type of near-invisible stitch. Shoulder pads and canvas are hand-cut and shaped to fit each individual wearer. Savile Row isn't only a sales pitch or a geographical location; for some it is a creed. The ASA didn't care. The Savile Row tailors lost the case.

When I ask Skinner what a Savile Row bespoke suit made to his standard would cost, he replies, "That's a question I'm often asked, and often I say if you can afford it, you shouldn't have to ask." He continues: "There's a certain kind of atmosphere that people expect. People don't expect to be discussed to other people. They come in here and there's not too many professions that allow physical touch, and people are putting their trust into you. People talk in fitting rooms. You can have intimate conversations with people and our customers know we use our discretion. What goes on between the walls of the fitting room stays there."

My audience is over. We shake hands and I find myself back on the sidewalk.

So, the price is a secret. That's okay. I've come ten thousand miles to be here to ask questions but still I have nothing to complain about. I'm in London. The sun is out. A giant Union Jack is fluttering in front of Gieves & Hawkes. I walk down the Row to find a place to sample steak and ale pie. A glamorous blonde in sunglasses, a beret, black leggings, and caramel-coloured boots – is it Claudia Schiffer? – walks by me and I smile stupidly at her. Then the sun blinks out. A thick cloud rolls in. The sky begins to spit rain. How very English.

The next day I head five doors down from Dege & Skinner to Henry Poole & Company, who are considered the founders of Savile Row. They too have dressed the Duke of

Wellington and Winston Churchill and, by some accounts, it was they who invented the tuxedo or dinner jacket.

In the basement works Paul Frearson. Frearson's greatest claim to fame is making Sean Connery's suits for all the James Bond films with the exception of Dr. No.

Frearson got his start as a tailor when he was twelve or thirteen years old. "At the time," he says, "there was an Edwardian trend where boys liked to taper their trousers. That was the fashion. So at school I wanted the narrow trousers. I got a needle and thread and, I don't know why, but I was able to narrow the trousers by hand and I wore them to school."

He was a sensation. People wanted to know where he had had them done. Soon enough, he was in business. For five shillings, he would alter boys' trousers. Then, at fifteen, he left school and took up an apprenticeship in Hastings, a seaside town in Sussex. It was not an affluent town and business was slow. He wanted to get away and he decided Savile Row was his ticket.

"I got a job at another establishment, a few doors down."

Frearson was unhappy there. Though bespoke, much of his work at the time was production line. He would have to do pockets or buttonholes all day long. He moved then from tailor shop to tailor shop, looking for an establishment that would allow him to create suits from start to finish. Like any great craftsman, he wanted artistic control. In 1963, he joined Anthony Sinclair, tailor to the stars and the creator of 007's Conduit Cut. It was a minimalist look that emphasized fit over pattern or colour.

"Connery was one of those people who could carry a nice suit."

Frearson is sixty-six. I ask him if he finds his work creatively satisfying. In reply, Frearson pulls out a bundle of wool smaller than a loaf of bread.

"That's how the job comes to me, you see," he said. "It's been cut and trimmed. Now I have to trim it, fix it, cut the canvasses. Put the coat together. I do everything. I give the pockets to the machiner, but I do everything else. It's my work. It has my label on it. My character. I get a feel-good factor out of it. Otherwise what's the point."

Frearson's intention is to keep on working for as long as he can. He calls retirement "expirement" and figures as long as his eyesight and dexterity hold up there is no reason for him to quit. But he knows the future is not his. Throughout his career, he has trained four apprentices. His last will be Rory Duffy.

Rory Duffy stands over six feet tall and has a puff of curly black hair that he tames into a part. His eyes are mischievous. He is the reason I have come to London. Duffy was the 2009 winner of the Golden Shears, a design contest open to young tailoring students and apprentices. He is twenty-seven years old and he represents the future.

Duffy's road to Savile Row began in the workshop of Joseph Martin Tailors in Sligo County, Ireland. The way Duffy speaks of his eighteen months there, the shop was populated by a Dickensian cast of characters. "One of the hand-finishers had polio as a kid," says Duffy. "He was not a happy man. He came across as old but he wasn't that old. He could never go upstairs so he had his own room downstairs while everyone else worked upstairs. Every day one of the female members of the staff would have to visit him and tell him the day's gossip. If no one came down by three p.m., he would become frustrated over his isolation and leave for the day."

Another colleague was Paddy the Presser. "If he went to the pub after work, he'd be gone for three days," Duffy said. "He would only come in for money." Once Duffy was trained to do Paddy's job the man was no longer allowed back in the shop.

"Then there was Jimmy. He was deaf and dumb. But he could communicate with Eugene Foley, the head tailor. Jimmy could make half a coat or at least that's all that Eugene let Jimmy make."

Often the older tailors would refuse to do certain jobs and much of it was passed on to Duffy. While vexing, the load and the diversity of work made Duffy versatile and quick.

Duffy was nineteen when he picked up a 1998 issue of *Clothing World*. He read an article about Henry Poole & Co.'s managing director Philip Parker, in which Parker talked about a drive to find sixteen-year-olds to train as tailors. Duffy first thought it was too late for him. But nevertheless he wrote down Parker's and the company's name on a piece of paper.

His chance to go to London came when a friend entered a reality TV show contest. His friend was in a glam rock band and Duffy was their sartorial roadie, providing thirty-four-inch-wide flared pants. With free time on his hands, he walked into Poole's off the street and asked for Philip Parker. Duffy was told to wait.

"I was half expecting an English dude with a finger up his ass but Philip wasn't like that at all," says Duffy. "It was like a slap on the back and down to earth. And I told him I worked for a tailor in Ireland and I wanted to come to this side of the pond."

Parker and Duffy spoke for an hour. Parker told him they would have space in a year for a new apprentice. He kept in contact with Parker and continued to make plans to move to London. When Duffy attempted to apply to the London College of Fashion's handcraft tailoring diploma program, he was told he was too late. Parker intervened on Duffy's behalf and his application was accepted. Every week for a hectic year, he spent two and a half days at the college, another day learning how to make trousers at another workshop, and Wednesdays at Poole's, where he started his in-house training with Paul Frearson.

There were early frictions between them. Frearson had difficulty understanding Duffy. "His accent, I found difficult to pick up," says Frearson. "It was embarrassing to keep saying 'pardon.' He had been accused of mumbling by other people, but it's not a problem because I've learned whatever he says is articulate. It was a matter of understanding each other."

Duffy then admits he played up his accent with Frearson. "Sometimes I'd say things in Gaelic really fast and he wouldn't be able to pick it up, and Paul would just say, 'Right.'"

Frearson wants me to know how groundbreaking Duffy is. He believes his former apprentice is the first Irishman ever to work at Poole's. Frearson looks at the younger man with a strange awe. "We work at it. You know, there's a generation gap."

"And Paul can't take a drink. If he has a pint, he's half cooked," says Duffy.

"I can't go to the pub. I'm on medication."

As they tease one another, both Frearson and Duffy continue to sew.

Chat, tea, radio, and now iPods provide degrees of relief from the monotony of tailoring. In a workshop, distractions are often welcome. Even the interruption of the shop boy with a set of new needles can inspire a conversation about appropriate gauge and length.

Tailoring can be genial work and is not often thought of as a dangerous occupation, but in 1794 the House of Lords had its concerns. As part of an inquiry into healthy work environments, the views of a French health investigator, a Monsieur Patissier, were entered into the record:

> As they [tailors] are almost constantly in a sitting posture, the body bent, with the head stooping forward, the blood is unequally distributed, and too large a quantity accumulates in the lungs, either because the bowels of the abdomen, compressed by the position of the body, admit of less blood, and which is therefore forced back into the vessels situated above, or because the short respirations of those who are sedentary, prevents the blood which enters the lungs from passing out with sufficient rapidity, by which local plethora in the heart and lungs is produced. In short, tailors are very liable to pulmonary phthisis, hydro-thorax, and haemoptysis, which often accompanies them to a very advanced age. . . . As the posture of the tailor causes the blood to flow into the upper part of the body, the circulation in the lower members is consequently much less active, which explains the emaciation and feebleness of the legs and thighs of this class of artisans, and the peculiar walk which distinguishes them.

I do not notice any strange gaits among the tailors at Poole's, but they do fidget. Sometimes Frearson stands and leans over his worktable, which they call a bench. Then he'll shift and turn his back to it. Often he uses a broken-down bentwood chair with no seat as a footstand. He will sit on his workbench and jam his feet into the bentwood hooks and loops, allowing him to raise or lower his legs. One might think tailoring is all in the hands, but legs and knees play a big role. A nice round knee makes for a good ham to give shape to a shoulder or collar a tailor is working on. One thigh can support an elbow and relieve some of the repetitive strain. Two thighs make a fine surface to baste up a back seam. In Victorian images of suit factories (making ready-made suits), one will find rows and rows of tailors sitting in classic cross-legged positions on tables, Buddha-like. The word *sartorial* is derived from this practice, as the tailor looks like a cross-legged satyr.

Nowadays, everyone is free to work and move as they see fit. Duffy mostly likes to stand. He has long slender fingers, the type one finds on piano players. They shake when he tries to thread a needle, but when he starts stitching, he is deft and quick. Frearson's pace is more steady.

They make quite the pair. One is near the end of his career. The other – so young in a field quickly growing grey with age – could walk out of here today, jump on a plane to anywhere, and find work before the day was done. All he would need to do is take off the jacket he made himself and pass it to his potential employer.

But, at least for now, Duffy and Frearson are still working

side by side, at either end of forty years. Here at Henry Poole & Co., the first of the great companies of bespoke tailoring on Savile Row, are two tailors, among the best in the world. They are bespoken.

I'VE MOSTLY THOUGHT OF MY CHILDHOOD AS A happy one despite the fact my mother disappeared for three nights after that first beating. When she returned, neither she nor my father spoke to any of the children about what happened. My mother never told us where she went, and we dared not ask. We treated the attack as if it were a hurricane. It came and destroyed and then dissipated. To speak of it would only invite the storm back.

To forgive is to forget and, in fact, I have very few memories of my childhood. Much of it is a blur. It's only now, as I try to come to terms with the past, that I realize I suffer from a kind of psyche-saving amnesia. I've forgotten in order to save myself. And what I do remember, what remains after the sifting, is golden.

By the time I was eleven, I had discovered the world beyond my family – and discovered how friendship could bring liberation. Out on the streets with other boys, I could ignore the confusion of home. At the time I kept a journal in ruled Hilroy exercise books. When I look back at these journals, I find no mentions of any household strife; instead there are snapshots of play and a running record of games I had learned or invented with my friends, most of which courted danger in one way or another. One was called underwater ping-pong. The game was played in the public pool up the street with as many neighbourhood children as we could find. Someone had to play the ball, and he or she would curl up and bob in the water while two teams attempted to push the human ball over designated goal lines. It was a desperate, clawing, and splashing contest. The only concession to safety was if the ball raised his or her hand, uncurled, and stood up. The teams would then have to stop until the human ball took a deep breath and returned to the playing position. From the lifeguard's chair, I'm sure it looked like a gang's attempt to drown someone.

Another game Paquito and I used to play involved our bikes. We would ride through the streets, pretending we were fighter planes. If you could keep your opponent's bike locked in the imaginary crosshairs in front of you, you scored a kill. Sometimes we dispensed with the ambiguity of pretend and played Kamikaze instead, which involved riding our bikes head on toward each other. When we were less than twenty yards apart, we would leap off and our unmanned bikes would collide. The last bike to fall was the winner.

The mock battles I had with Paquito made sense compared to the fights my parents had. Battles were meant to be about adventure and bravery. We made swords out of broken hockey sticks and used garbage can lids for shields. Out with Paquito, I don't remember feeling scared or even anxious. My family was the furthest thing from my mind.

Night was a different matter, especially in the littoral zone between wakefulness and sleep. A feeling of dread always came over me then. In my bedroom, lying flat on my bed, I remember trying to expand my consciousness the way the heroes in the comic books I read could. Marvel Comics' Captain Mar-Vell, an alien warrior spy who eventually becomes Earth's defender, had the power of cosmic awareness that manifested itself in a keen ability to detect the unseen and the near future. I used my powers to determine the state of inebriation my father would be in when he finally came home: happy and sober; happy and drunk; unhappy and sober yet intent on getting drunk at home; miserable and drunk. How the car entered the driveway, how the front door creaked, how heavy or light his footfalls were when he came through the door – these told me everything about how the night would go.

I would occasionally put my ear to my parents' bedroom wall and listen to them murmur to each other in bed. Sometimes there were sobs – my father could say cruel things to my mother even as they shared the same bed. Other times I heard giggles, quick breaths, and sighs of what I now believe must have been furtive love-making. There is a literary and psychological trope that says thinking of your parents having sex leads to some form of trauma, but I recall feeling only relief whenever I heard those sounds. I preferred silence. Nothing bad could happen if everyone was asleep. The peaceful nights were rare.

In 1980, my father suffered another setback. The Sheraton Mount Royal was going to be converted into condominiums. The Kon-Tiki was closing. The news was crushing. Restaurants were his home, and the people at the lounge with whom he sat around the bar after the kitchen had been cleaned and all the receipts counted – they were his real family. Though he loved us, he really couldn't relate to the strange collection of children that waited for him at home, he couldn't make peace with us. He had no memory of his own father and therefore no role model for how to be a father to the four of us. It's so clear to me now. When he was little more than a boy he had left home to live and work at the Dragon Room Inn, sleeping on a cot in a room over the restaurant. To most people this might sound like a hardship, but for my father the restaurant was where he found comfort and a sense of belonging. But the Dragon Room was no more, and soon there would be no Kon-Tiki either.

The parent company had offered my father a job at its head office in Chicago but he refused it. It may have been for us, the children. He may have felt relocating would be too hard. It would have been a regular job though, one without the odd hours of a restaurant manager. And maybe it would have saved him.

This is the period in my childhood when I began to see how alcohol was taking him from us, from me. He became erratic. Even when he did come home early, he was usually in a foul mood. My father would clump into the house, silent and grim. He complained about how the house was a mess. He complained about supper being late. My mother would bark back sarcastically, "How would you know."

Sometimes that was enough to launch him into a yelling match with my mother, but mostly I remember him going down into the basement, turning up the stereo, and playing records so loud the floors shook. I can still hear Nana Mouskouri's *Songs of the British Isles* rumbling through the floor: "Why should I act such a childish part, and love a man that will break my heart?" He would put on albums my mother used to play as lullabies for the children when we were babies. It was awful to hear the songs corrupted, played at such a howling volume that they not only took away my sleep but seemed to reach back through time and rattle the spindles of my crib.

My father would sit on or lie under the ping-pong table next to the stereo and play these records as we ate dinner without him upstairs and then prepared to go to sleep. To this day, I remember the feeling of lying in bed, listening to the final song on the album, "I Gave My Love a Cherry," and hoping, as the tune faded, that he would have finally passed out. If not, the music would go on all night. No one could make him stop or go to sleep. All we could do was wait him out. I can see the needle rolling past the last song and the record turning and turning with great bumps and hisses. I would have to tiptoe around his limbs to retrieve the needle and turn down the volume. Only then would the house have the mercy of silence.

These are hard and sharp memories to recall, but there were many nights when I was free of anxiety. In the summer of 1981, my father gave me a copy of Carl Sagan's book on space, *Cosmos*. I'm not sure why. I suppose he wanted to spark in me a sense of wonder, or perhaps he wanted to foster my appreciation of science, but he never took me out for a walk in the country on a clear night to point up to the stars and name the constellations. That's what I wanted, but even then I knew it was impossible for him to give me this. All he had to offer me was Carl Sagan. Which was nearly enough. With *Cosmos* I was able to time the arrival of the Perseid meteor shower in mid-August. The book detailed how Perseid would offer a shooting star every minute. At around eleven p.m., I pulled a cot out onto the driveway and lay under a blanket and stared up at the night sky. Under the sky, my family's problems seemed blissfully distant and small, and with each streak of light I made a wish for them to stay that way.

AT THE SHOP, I CONTINUE MY CAMPAIGN TO MASTER straight stitching on the old Singer. I sit at the machine and sew hundreds, thousands of stitches, stopping, going, making ninety-degree turns, all in an effort to get a feel for the pedal control. It sounds maddening, but it is soothing. In it I find solace.

I came into this apprenticeship with the hopes of becoming the person to carry on the Modernize Tailors legacy with the blessing of Bill, Jack, and the Wong family. I saw myself becoming the tailor of choice for all the indie music bands, young architects, and writers I have come across in my life. I'd hold mini fashion shows and perhaps start a line of ready-wear clothes. I would be The Man. Bringing guys over to play poker in the back, I'd have a stash of cognac I would haul out and we'd smoke cigars and impress ourselves with how manly we were.

But now that I've spent time here, and watched the sun glint through the windows after a rain shower and ignite the colours on the bolts of wool along the wall, I wish things could stay exactly the way they are. I love the way Park and Laddie tune into two different radio stations and somehow the news and the soft pop rock songs meld beautifully with the thrum of the sewing machines. I love the button jars and the blue box of pins and razor blades. I love the soft thump of the iron and the scrape of a stool leg on the concrete floor. Most of all, I love Bill.

More than just teaching me how to sew, Bill and I have talked about many things. He has told me about his family and about his own father. Bill's father emigrated from China to Canada in 1912. He started as a houseboy and fell in with an old English tailor who taught him the trade. He then opened his own shop, Modernize. By the time Bill was born in 1922, his father had turned it into a thriving enterprise serving farmers, loggers, and miners. Back then, everybody wore suits when in town.

Bill and Jack grew up in the shop. Their father let them play with the scraps and spools around Modernize as toddlers, and later he let them help with sewing buttons, making slacks, and hemming skirts. But their father felt the boys could do better. In 1942, he sent Jack to university to study civil engineering and Bill went into mechanical engineering. When the war was over, they graduated. But when a city hall recruiter came to campus in search of new hires, both Bill and Jack were told not to apply. Standing in front of the entire graduating class of engineers, the recruiter said, "Tell the Chinese boys in the back not to bother or we'll all be embarrassed."

That was how Bill became a tailor. Maybe he retreated to the shop when what he really should have done was walk up to the front of the lecture hall and popped the man in the mouth. But that's a fantasy. Bill was told he did not belong and he fell back into the life he knew. His father didn't want Bill to work there. But Bill realized then what I have discovered now: people still need a tailor, even if that tailor is only an alterationist who couldn't cut a suit to save his or her life. The hemming, hole-patching, zipper-replacing, and button-anchoring miracles the most modest tailor can provide do one great important thing: clothes that are generic and literally run-of-the-mill are converted with a few nips and tucks into garments for distinct individuals. Tailors make people feel special and valued. Tailors are wanted. Unlike a mechanical engineer, tailors touch people's lives, figuratively speaking, though the literal touch is also quite soothing in a deep way. Every measure, every detail conferred upon the dangerous yet trust-building exercise of pinning strokes the ego and feeds the soul. Bill knows this. Though he's in his eighties, he doesn't want to retire, and that's a good thing. Modernize Tailors is where he belongs and he is lucky to know it.

My calling, my destiny, however, is still in doubt. So far, I've worked on an article of clothing for a paying customer only once. One day, Bill taps me on the shoulders and tells me I have to narrow some pants for a gentleman.

I am suspicious. The pants have a waist size of twenty-six inches. They are made out of stretch denim. There is no way a man would wear these. I am certain I am being hazed. They know I will screw up and they are going to give me a hard time about it.

Bill says, "You have to take in the legs. Two inches."

Bill drops his finger on the pants to show how much needs to come off the inseam.

Two inches, right. That would leave less than nine inches' circumference for the pant leg. Hardly enough room to even squeeze through a foot. It has to be a gag.

I grab the largest scissors I can find. They weigh about five pounds and the blades are fourteen inches long. I am going to call Bill's bluff. I'm going to cut the pants in half, horizontally. I open the blades, ready to saw off the prank at the knees, when the skinniest man in the world walks into the shop. He has a pompadour and a chain attached to his wallet. His T-shirt has holes in it. He is a hipster-barber from down the block and his name is Nick. He has a twenty-six-inch waist. He has come to try on his pants.

If you ever decide to become a client here, you should know we don't have an office manager or a quality assurance process. Modernize Tailors has no scheduler or scheduling software. There is no computer. The calendars lying around the shop are haphazard freebies grabbed from different stores and suppliers. Some show the wrong month, even the wrong year. Obedience to the timestream is optional here, and customers should call before coming to the shop to pick stuff up.

Bill says, "Just a second."

I jump into Bill's workstation and drop the straight stitcher's foot down. It is do or die. I put pressure down on the pedal carefully. The needle moves up one leg slowly and surely, taking the flabbergasting two inches off the inseam. After negotiating the thick folds of denim near the crotch, I guide the needle down the other leg. I am tailoring for a living, at the service of a slightly irate customer with the waistline of a teenage girl. I decide to speed things up and finish off with a firm, masterful flourish by racing through the last few inches. I put a bit more weight on the pedal. The throat of the motor emits a high-speed growl. It is the sound of an F1 Honda racing engine. The needle has gone into Gatling gun mode, but instead of spitting bullets it is a furious rattling of stitches — 1,300 stitches per minute. The machine grabs the pant leg with its teeth. I panic. I put more pressure on the pedal. Fifty stitches hammer into one spot on the calf. I know if I pull the threads away there will be a hole.

Nick looks askance. Bill taps me on the shoulder. I slide off the stool to let him finish the job. Bill pulls the pants out and resets the needle. He stitches a fine straight line an eighth of an inch from my erratic effort and skirts by my disaster zone. An easy save for Bill.

He hands the pants to Nick. The young man disappears into the dressing room. When he comes out, the pants are clinging to his thighs and calves but still he tugs at them. "Can you take it in any more?"

When Nick leaves I turn to Bill. "Don't ever do that to me again."

"What?"

"That was a real customer."

"Well, that's what I said."

I go back to my machine. It's true I need to start doing more of the real work of becoming a tailor. I need to focus. I need to master the basic skills. For all its comforts, the shop is a place of business. Every button, every snip, every em-dash of thread I make is meant to bring me closer to where Bill is now.

Later that evening, after Jack and Park have left, I saunter to the back and pull up a stool beside Bill. We are the only two left in the shop. I ask, "Why do you keep me around?"

Bill turns away from the newspaper he is reading and stretches his arm out and puts his hand on my shoulder. "JJ, if you can sew, with your background in architecture and design, you can do anything."

It is the kind of thing only a parent could tell you, that little lie or shot of blind optimism to keep you going. Sure, a friend or a spouse can say the same thing, but it doesn't have the same effect. It's just different. Not that I'm familiar with these kinds of intergenerational man-to-man chats. My father never said anything like that to me, and when I was ready to engage with him as a man we never had the chance.

"Bill, were you close to your father?"

"Sure, we were close."

"I mean, were you square with him when he died? Did you feel you were together?"

"Of course. But not affectionate. We didn't hug or anything. It's not the Chinese way. But I remember, when Jack and I were young, we would go to English school all day, then go to Chinese school, and after that we would work at Modernize until late with my father. I don't think any other kids worked like us. Then at ten o'clock, we would come home and my father would make us a steak. A porterhouse."

"You remember the cut."

"Of course, I do. Medium-rare on a white plate."

"Porcelain?" I don't know why I needed to take in all the details. But I can see them in the kitchen. It's late. For some reason I imagine floral wallpaper. There's a raw bulb over the kitchen table. And the steak on a white plate is in the middle.

"That's it. With just a steak on it. He always wore a suit. He didn't own any jeans or T-shirts. He would put on an apron and fry us a steak with ginger, garlic, and soy sauce."

Bill looks down at the newspaper in front of him. After a paragraph or two he says, "Yeah, we were close."

"Bill, why did you take me on as an apprentice?"

"I'll take whatever comes my way. These days I have to. I thought you might add something to the place."

"Did you know what you were getting into when you took me in?"

"In the beginning, I knew it was going to be tough going. But once I made up my mind to take you on, well, I have to do my best to carry on. I can't quit halfway."

"Do you think I can make it as a tailor?"

"You would know best yourself. I hope you realize there's a lot of hard work in tailoring. It's very hard. Not everybody can do it. You can be a janitor and get better pay. One person who used to work here became a painter. He had a nice touch for painting trim. But don't worry. You're doing the job for me. You've done a big favour for me."

"Yeah, but, how do you feel about having me around?"

"Well, you're good for business."

For some reason, what Bill just said hurts.

I DIDN'T SEE MUCH OF MY FATHER DURING THE
winter of 1981, but one night he came into my room and
woke me, his cold hands shaking my shoulders. He was
drunk. I had, in my optimism, expected food – maybe
seafood chow mein or snails in black bean sauce or, better
yet, Ben's smoked meat sandwiches – but all he wanted was
my help. He'd noticed there was something wrong with the
front door. A screw was missing from the strike plate. At one
in the morning he wanted to fix it and he needed me to
hold the plate up. I stood by the front door in my pyjamas,
shivering as the cold winter air blew in. He grabbed a
screwdriver and a screw and began to ram the point of the
screw through the hole and into the wood. He didn't bother
to drill a hole or use an awl to make a starting point. He just
rammed the screw into the jamb. For a moment I marvelled
at his strength, but after a few twists my heart sank. The
screw began to go in wrong. I told him it was sideways. His
face went red. His eyes were already bloodshot. There was a

smear of oil from his skin on his aviator glasses. He said, "Fuck," and then continued to drive the screw into the door jamb until it wouldn't go in any farther. Then he dropped the screwdriver onto the foyer floor and stood up and fumed. His breathing was heavy, and his shoulders rose up and down. He looked confused and sad. On the floor, a dirty puddle of melted snow had formed around his galoshes. It was so ridiculous and pathetic. I looked at him and something changed inside me. I was no longer afraid of him, but I was afraid I would become like him.

He shambled down to the basement to play his music. Left standing by the front door, I examined the screw head. It reminded me of what a flying saucer might look like if it crashed to Earth, half buried, a monument to its own ruin.

I shut the door and turned out the lights.

My father must have been very drunk that night. He played only one side of a record before passing out.

When I slipped back into bed, I lay on my back and crossed my arms over my chest and listened to the house. Lenny gave a little cough in the next room. In their room, Aimee and Tammy murmured to each other for a few more minutes before they too drifted off. My mother was safely in her bed. The refrigerator cycled off. The furnace clicked on. I lay in my bed and began to imagine what it would be like to travel to another planet and leave this one far, far behind.

WITH ALL THE CUTTING, STITCHING, AND SLICING a tailor does, the work is similar to that of an ER doctor: the bulk of our trade at the shop is to repair and revive. At Modernize, the delicate operations are carried out on the big table in the back. The workbench is about six feet wide and sixteen feet long, and a well-worn canvas padding covers the entire surface. Besides being a place to baste and hand-finish garments under a bright band of neon lights, it is used as a giant pin cushion and ironing board. Bill, Jack, Park, and Laddie sit on only one side of the bench in a narrow space, crammed with a quartet of stools. The floor is littered with dropped pins, safety razors, threads, and scraps of wool and interlinings. The tailors at the bench work with their sewing machines to their backs.

Tailors have to handle their share of emergencies. Men have walked in with missing buttons on their jackets or ripped seams in their only pair of suit pants that they have to wear for a wedding or an important job interview the next day. Sometimes, there is only so much we can do.

One man stands out in my mind. His name was Jonathan and he walked in clutching a beat-up three-piece suit. He didn't just dump the coat on the table and tell Bill he needed it altered to fit him. No, Jonathan had a story. He placed the suit on the cutting table and opened it up so we could see the lining.

"I'm getting married," Jonathan said. "This is the suit my father came over from Italy in and I'd like to wear it."

"Try it on," said Bill, holding the jacket up. "Jonathan's not a very Italian name."

"I know," said Jonathan. "My dad just liked the sound of it."

"More English."

"I guess so."

Jonathan was tall and skinny, with a hawkish nose, close-set eyes, and a soft baritone voice. His father must have been a labourer. The suit was well made, with a light amount of padding typical in Italian suits, but the cut was full. Jonathan's father was a husky man. The unbuttoned front of the suit swung loosely like a pair of giant shutters. Bill called over Park, master of coatmaking.

Park pulled at the flapping front. "Can't do it."

He indicated the only way to attack the problem was with a radical recutting of the lapels. "If I make it smaller, it will make the pockets on the front come together."

Bill tugged at the side and back seams, searching for other spots from which to remove the extra fabric. Park shook his head and waved his hands, dismissing the thought, "Not enough," then returned to his station.

Jonathan looked at Bill with an imploring expression. "We can make you a new suit," said Bill.

"I'll pay you anything," said Jonathan.

Bill could have taken Jonathan's money but the alteration would have resulted in an absurd suit. "I'm sorry," said Bill.

Jonathan slipped out of the jacket and thanked all of us, a strained, desperate look on his face. He left with his father's suit clenched in white-knuckled hands.

When making an entirely new suit, a tailor creates something unique from the featureless, dark sameness of a bolt. From it he draws thirty-four distinct shapes on the wool that, once cut out, reveal little of how they are to come together again. As a result, a tailor must be careful and work in meticulous stages. There are parts of the suit that don't fit together well and yet they must. This is the strange by-product of trying to shape flat, albeit very pliant, fabric over the complex geometry of the body. A good example is the back of a suit jacket, which is cut wider than the front to accommodate the fullness of dorsal muscles and a man's slight forward hunch. As the back piece reaches around the neck and over the shoulders to meet the front of the suit, one discovers quickly that the back piece is more than an inch wider than the front piece at the connecting seam. A tailor has to carefully gather the extra material at the back and join it smoothly to the front without creating clumsy rows of wavy pin tucks. Technique matters.

But I am learning that tailoring is not all technique and no style.

Sometimes Bill doesn't want me to sew or clean or stack the magazines or sort out the bolts. Instead, he wants me to watch Park. My perch is across from him on the civilian side of the workbench. As is his way, Park doesn't look at me and hardly speaks, and I am expected to respect the silence.

Park is thin and wears glasses. His hair is slicked back and streaked with grey. While Bill and Jack tend to shuffle, Park carries himself like a dancer. Many tailors, before getting into the rhythm of sewing, have shaky hands as they thread or sink a needle into the fabric. Not Park. The coatmaker-in-chief at Modernize conducts his business with speed and precision. When he sews he draws on the thread crisply but not too hard, since a tight stitch will pucker the fabric. Even when he snips away thread or fabric, he does it with a musical snap.

Though he labours hard and his speed is the result of years of practice, Park embodies the creative gratification I am looking for. With tailoring, an idea or vision can come into the mind, be sketched, and then diagrammed quickly. It can be a swift act of bravura compared to architecture, where there are design and building permits, layers of consulting engineers, a client whom the architect pains with his or her presence as much as serves. Many things can go wrong with an architect's best-laid plans. Fashion failures are only aesthetic ones. An architectural failure can bury souls in depths of concrete.

And besides, can an architect, slumped in his ergonomic chair, clicking away on the mouse, shuffling through the multiple layers of AutoCAD drawings, truly move with the grace that Park does?

Park holds himself like a man who knows exactly what he has to do. His hands stay close to his body; he rarely stretches out. Park keeps his movements and threads short. Longer threads just get in the way and can form unwanted knots or catch on other items on the bench. Park pulls the needle in quick, economical motions. When he needs to use the soap to mark a line, the fingers on his right hand arrange themselves into a bird's head: the waxy white bar becomes the beak and he pecks a crisp, even dashed line. The only time he extends himself is when he irons. The iron, which is ten times heavier than a domestic iron and is set on the highest temperature possible, sits on a steel pad with insulation underneath it. The only thing keeping the heat from scorching the wool is a heat-resistant fabric sleeve over the pressure plate. When Park uses it, he floats his left hand over the jacket while his right hand guides the iron as it slowly sails across the wavy surface of the wool like a stately ocean liner, leaving in its path a smooth sea of calm. When he's done, Park docks the iron back on the pad with a firm punctuating thump.

A tailor can sew with style and Park has it. But it is a performance conducted every day without an audience.

Who passeth by a myrtle bush, and plucketh not a twig,
O may he not enjoy his youth, although he's tall and big.

Greek rhyme from the Island of Chios

MY FATHER DID NOT LIKE LAPEL FLOWERS OR BOU-
tonnieres. While he admired Pierre Trudeau, Canada's prime
minister at the time, my father felt the gallant politician's
signature red rose was too effeminate. This might explain
why the lapel buttonhole on my father's suit remains closed.
The buttonhole threads are there. There are two parallel rows
of raised stitches that look like little arrowheads dotting
around the buttonhole, but there is no hole through which
a flower stem could be passed.

Looking at it though, I realize the answer to my problem
of how to fix the width of my father's lapels has been in
front of me all along. The lapel buttonhole. If I trim the
lapel with the intention of retaining the original buttonhole, I may as well not bother at all. The difference would
be marginal. But if I want to make the lapels thinner
and correct the proportions, then I will have to cut beyond
the notional hole. There's no way around it. Committed,
I baste the correct line, then lay the jacket on the living

room floor and trim off nearly two inches from the lapels.

With the lapels cut, the inner workings of the suit are exposed. If you ever decide to try this at home, be aware that you never know what you're going to find inside.

Tailors are famous for stuffing all sorts of materials inside a jacket to give a man's chest the right shape, including horsehair, canvas, and felt. Unethical or enterprising (you decide) coatmakers have also been known to stitch into the lining cutting-room scraps, old upholstery, even seat padding. This extra material, collectively known as the canvas, gives the suit its body so even when unworn the suit maintains some of the same form as when someone is wearing it. The canvas also helps the lapels to keep their shape and aids in creating the sexy curve of the lapel roll as it turns inside out. Even the more dubious materials are forgivable so long as the lapels, once properly sewn, have a nice roll.

To give the lapel the fullest, softest, most sensual shape, the canvas needs to be pad-stitched. Pad-stitching is superior because it guarantees that a tailor, or a very specialized machine, has carefully curled your lapel as the canvas was attached. In the cruder production-line process, the interlining is often glued into a jacket while it lies flat. Then the lapel will be folded rather than rolled. Folded-over lapels are sterile, sharp-edged, and, I suggest, less sensual. Curled lapels look and sit better on the chest. They feel amazing.

To tell the difference while shopping for an off-the-rack suit, simply pull at the lapel and chest fabric. If you detect an independent middle layer inside, then you have a classic floating canvas pad-stitched into the jacket. If your jacket doesn't have an inner third layer, I'm not saying don't buy it, just don't pay more than $800 for a suit that has been glued or, rather, tailored with heat-activated adhesives.

Guess what I find inside my father's suit? It isn't an elegant floating canvas. No, when I cut into the lapels old bits of dry glue explode into small puffs of dust. When I peel the two layers of wool apart, I find synthetic fibres and foam padding. I can't remove the fusibles, but I rip out the foam layer and decide to replace it with cotton. Once I stuff the new layer in, I carefully work my way up and down the lapel, anchoring it with near invisible prick stitches. When it's all over, the lapel comes to life. Instead of looking like it has been bent by a sheet metal press, the lapel blooms out, soft, organic, enticing to the hand and eye. I also put in a new buttonhole. And it won't be a faux hole. On many current suits, the buttonhole is merely notional, a concentration of thread on the left side to suggest a buttonhole where there is no actual hole at all. Faux or real, a good lapel needs one. On a graphic level, the lapel buttonhole serves as a compositional device: with the notches and peaks of lapels, and the bracing horizontal of the breast pocket, the lapel buttonhole encourages the eye to move upwards towards the face instead of following the V-shaped downward plunge of the exposed shirt. It's always better if the buttonhole is functional, because, unlike my father, I think the boutonniere is a beautiful thing.

I would like to say the wearing of a boutonniere is a lost art, but even during its heyday at the end of the nineteenth century, it was considered fey. One famous wearer, the ultra-chic Boniface, Marquis de Castellane, was described in *A History of Men's Fashion* by Farid Chenoune as a man with "affected gestures and manners." Chenoune cites one contemporary who wrote that Boniface smelled of "Versailles, hair powder, lace and cream of orris root."

I think it's a shame men don't call upon the buttonhole more often. It's not as if wearing lapel flowers is bad etiquette. In fact it's quite proper – men still have to wear them at weddings and proms. Unfortunately, when the time comes, the execution is often poor. The last boutonniere I wore at a wedding was a white rose, which is fine on its own, but it was also accompanied by baby's breath, fern-like sprigs, and other miscellaneous flora like laurel leaf. To hold this tossed salad together, the flower was pierced by metal wires and the rest affixed by a gooey ribbon tape. The boutonniere was over-designed. Too heavy, too big, and just too much; it was a case of idle hands becoming the devil's tools. The flower kept drooping down. Worse yet, the construction was so thick with adhesive that the stem couldn't fit through the buttonhole. Stop the madness! For a wedding, nothing more is required than a bunch of flowers to be shared by all the male members of a party as they dress. In such a scenario, I recommend the best man should have the job of keeping a penknife handy. When the struggle with the bow ties is done (if tuxedos are being worn), the groom or best man can make available a bottle of Irish whiskey (God, not Scotch, please) for a quick snarf. Once the toasts are done, the groom and his men can set to cutting a flower from the bunch for their lapels.

The perfect flower is small, fresh, and just opening. The bloom should be no wider than the jacket's lapel unless you wear oversized red shoes and yellow pants and your name is Bozo. The flower's scale should relate well to the size of the tie knot and the volume of the pocket puff showing out of the breast pocket, but avoid having the trio of flower, knot, and puff be exactly the same size or they will begin to look too crowded; instead, for an easy fix, fold the handkerchief into a square and show just a small edge of it. Or simply dispense with one of the elements if etiquette allows it. We're not trying to win the Trifecta here, fellas.

For a stellar overall effect, a degree of nonchalance must be conveyed in the wearing of a boutonniere. The flower has to look like an inspired improvisation.

Take as a role model the first person who is said to have introduced the tradition of wearing a boutonniere for a wedding: Prince Albert, husband of Queen Victoria. According to the often repeated story, immediately after their wedding ceremony in 1840, the twenty-year-old Queen Victoria (who made it henceforth de rigueur for royal brides to wear white) was riding in a carriage with her new husband when she gave him a flower from her wedding bouquet of myrtle – a small, white, five-petalled flower with a spray of stamen. The Prince is said to have then gallantly cut into the breast of his jacket with his penknife to accommodate the myrtle. This is pure balderdash. On his wedding day, Prince Albert wore the formal dress of an English field marshal: a red tailcoat (short in the front and long in the back, like a mullet, with no lapels), white knee-length breeches, and large white satin rosettes on his shoulder. The thought of Albert, a German prince, slicing an English military uniform is fanciful and would have made a terrible start for his career as an Imperial consort.

However, I have an alternative theory. It is possible that on the day following their wedding, as they made their way to Windsor Castle for a short honeymoon, Prince Albert cut a hole in the lapel of his dark travelling suit. On this same day, their only twenty-four-hour window of privacy, the young bride would write in her diary, "Already the 2nd day since our marriage; his love and gentleness is beyond every-thing, and to kiss that dear soft cheek, to press my lips to his, is heavenly bliss."

Regardless of which piece of apocrypha one chooses to believe, it should be noted Prince Albert was not the first boutonniere dandy. Nosegays, posies, and other small bunches of flowers are depicted sitting in unbuttoned lapel holes in paintings dating from the eighteenth century. Thomas Gainsborough painted a portrait of Captain William Wade in 1771 featuring a large eruption of blooms coming out of the officer's red coat, more than fifty years before Prince Albert's romantic alteration.

There were also the Macaronis of 1772, a foppish group of young male Italophiles who were as notorious as the Merry Gang. Often referred to as a club, the Macaronis were a subculture of homosexuals in London who had collected around a publicly castigated sodomite with the unfortunate name of Drybutter. They were easily recognized by their "tight-fitting vests, cinnamon knee-breeches and striped stockings." They wore "monumental wigs" and enormous amounts of flowers in multiple buttonholes. The Macaronis, as fashion figures, fascinated many of their contemporaries: they appear in the literary works of Horace Walpole; Samuel Johnson took a direct interest in Drybutter's legal problems (he was eventually executed for forgery); printmakers Matthew and Mary Darly published a popular series of satirical caricatures of notable public figures dressed as Macaronis; the press made the Macaronis the punchline of lewd jokes in its coverage of the sodomy trial; and of course the Macaronis survive to this day in the lyrics to the old song "Yankee Doodle Dandy."

But none of this history mattered a lick to Prince Albert's bride. On the day he may have cut a hole in his jacket breast, Queen Victoria wrote to her Uncle Leopold, the King of Belgium, "Really, I do not think it possible for any one in the world to be happier, or as happy as I am. He is an Angel, and his kindness and affection for me is really touching. To look in those dear eyes, and that dear sunny face, is enough to make me adore him."

What we know for sure is that before her return to London, Victoria ordered myrtle cuttings from her bouquet planted in the gardens of Windsor Castle. Since then, royal brides have carried in their wedding bouquets sprigs of myrtle descended from the original bush.

On New Year's Eve, 1981, my father had a surprise for my mother. He told her to fix herself up because they were going out to celebrate. He watched my mother put on a green silk cheongsam dress embroidered with peonies. It was a favourite of his. The hem of the dress fell to her ankles but the side vents of the skirt rose daringly high up the sides.

My father wore a dark blue three-piece suit with a dark tie that had tiny dots – not large, crude polka dots, but Lipton dots, the kind you would find on Winston Churchill's ties. On his shirt cuffs, he added eighteen-karat gold links with jade settings that matched my mother's dress. He then presented her with an orchid, which he slipped onto her left wrist. Then she put on a mink coat and they were off.

I can imagine my mother cosseting the orchid, protecting it from being crushed by the mink's heavy fur sleeves. Though my father liked to lavish luxuries on her, she never claimed to want them. It wasn't a false restraint. She was indifferent and simply took what she was given in stride. She often let me play with the big pelt. I would wear the giant mink and roar about the house trying to eat Aimee and Lenny. To my mother, the mink was just another coat, but the flower was different. She took real pleasure in piercing avocado pits with skewers and mounting them on glasses filled with water so she could tease out a sprout. For my mother, the gift of a flower from my father would have been precious. My father, a child of the city, had no green thumb himself but he understood the power of flowers. He gave my mother an orchid on every wedding anniversary, Valentine's Day, Mother's Day, and birthday. He gave her orchids the first time they attended a high school dance together as young teens and now, after a decade of marriage and four children, those orchids kept fresh the memory of early romance.

My father took my mother downtown on New Year's Eve in his Oldsmobile 88. My mother never once saw my father park his car whenever they went out at night. He could drive up to any major hotel or fine restaurant in the city – even if he wasn't spending the evening there – and always find a valet who would greet him with a "Hello, John." My father would toss his keys straight up into the air and the valet would slip underneath just in time to catch them.

That night their destination was Club 737, on the top floor of Place Ville Marie. He had reserved a table by the window because he knew the view from the tallest building in the city would astonish her. My father always ordered for her. They ate smoked salmon and duck à l'orange with lemon wedges, and he showed her how to squeeze the juice by pulling tight the small cloth bows knotted around the wedges. It was so the juice wouldn't run onto her fingers, he explained. They drank wine, a Chablis Grand Crus Les Preuses. "I love you more than anyone else in the world," he told her. "I love the children, but I love you more."

"And I love you," she replied. "But I love the children more because they need me. They need me more than you do."

Later they danced to a jazz trio with a singer. They weren't dancers, but my father put his hands on the small of her waist and my mother draped her forearms around his neck and together they shuffled like teenagers at a high school prom. When more experienced couples began to come onto the dance floor, my parents drew closer together, their bodies touching, swaying against one another through the silk and wool. They were still young. Ten years younger than I am now. The other dancers, much older than my parents, gave them space on the floor. Despite all the hurt between them, my father and mother still believed they were in love.

ALL FASHION, YES, EVEN SUIT WEARING, HAS A death-match, Mad-Max-in-the-Thunderdome aspect to it. Clothes can be risky business. You are putting yourself out there with what you wear. Your clothes are saying something about you. You may be attacked from the conservative front, those pillars of etiquette and custom. Or you may take broadsides from the arbiters of style, who would squash you with their spike-heeled Louboutins. And they're everywhere. They're in the newspapers, online, and in the cubicle beside you.

If you choose to dress with any sort of intention or sense of purpose — with *style* — you really can't win. That's why people who take risks with the way they dress are thought of as brave. Get used to the fashion police. God help me, I'm one of them. I can't stand to see men walking around in suits with all their buttons fastened. I can barely keep myself from walking up to them and showing them how it's done.

If you don't know, two-button coats like my father's should follow the Always-Never rule: the top button should always be closed, while the bottom button never. A fastened bottom button is considered poor form. On a three-button suit, the matter is more complicated. Many three-button suits have very high and firm lapels. The top button should only be closed if the lapels are so rigid and flat that they demand to be closed. On a softer-lapelled three-button coat, the lapel may roll past the top button and only use of the middle or "always" button is required. Again, the bottom button is the "never" button. In other words, the rule for three-button coats goes Sometimes-Always-Never.

A man who buttons all his buttons is, I hate to say it, conspicuous to those with greater sartorial experience. It won't matter if he spends $5,000 on the get-up, he will be pitied. It's harsh, it's cruel. One may consider it a triumph of taste and cultivation over wealth and power, but it is also snobbery.

I have another confession to make. My father's suit isn't even a real suit. It's more accurately described as a blazer suit, which is an oxymoron. Suits imply a coordinated set of matched garments – jacket and pants and sometimes a vest. A blazer is a sporting jacket that is meant to be paired with unmatched pants, like khakis or flannels.

A blazer should never be mistaken for a suit coat. A blazer has patch pockets, while a suit has pockets discretely hidden in the lining and tucked under flaps. A suit conveys a sense of honest toil – that's why most people call them business suits (though, ironically, they were formerly known as lounge suits). The blazer hardly exudes the same probity and authority. Blazers suggest a life of shameless privilege without the stain of hard labour. They can summon visions of exclusive oak-walled billiard rooms, briar pipes, the pink pages of the *Financial Times*, and general idleness. Blazers are lax. And taking the extra step to match one with a pair of pants, to transform it into a blazer suit like my father's, does nothing to ameliorate the situation. It only makes the blazer more confounding.

William Thourlby brings the blazer suit conundrum most sharply into focus. The actor who first portrayed the Marlboro Man back in the 1950s, Thourlby was also one of the first corporate image consultants, and he had nothing good to say about the blazer suit: "Suits are traditionally recognized for situations of a serious nature. Sport coats are for less serious occasions. The blazer suit, a hybrid of the two, is neither fish nor fowl. Consequently, it is seldom appropriate for either situation and incongruous in most. The blazer suit has almost as many negative connotations as the leisure suit. The blazer suit is a blatant attempt to sacrifice good taste and tradition for economy."

It would seem my father's suit is not a suit at all. As with my grey ghillie suit, I have once again fallen in with a chimera. But should I give up the cause based on the opinion of one man?

There is a biting sneer in Thourlby's assessment that is intended to put the matter to rest, as if the evocation of good taste will pierce the tawdry dragon of economy through the heart and exsanguinate it once and for all. Part of me wants to tell William Thourlby to fuck off.

Thourlby, however, is only a minor figure in the

pantheon of style arbiters. The man who stands above all others in this strange branch of human endeavour is George Bryan "Beau" Brummell. Born in 1778, Brummell was anointed by one satirist as "the greatest professor of two of the most popular sciences – Dress and Affectation."

Many biographers choose to accentuate his humble beginnings, but the social standing of Brummell's family was such that he attended Eton College at the age of twelve. There he began to build his reputation for fastidious manners and cutting remarks. One satirical sketch claims Brummell broke off pursuit of a beautiful niece of a colonel because "she asked for soup twice" at dinner. After Eton, Brummell went to Oxford, where he dispensed with academic ambitions and instead became a professional climber of the social ladder. In 1794, after a year at Oxford, he dropped out and, with the inheritance from his father, he purchased a junior army commission with the 10th Hussars. While this may seem like a radical change of direction for Brummell, it was not. The unit was "the most expensive, the most impertinent, the best-dressed, the worst-moraled regiment in the British army." The foppish 10th was ceremonially commanded by George, Prince of Wales. And it was not long before Brummell, who appeared as a "slight but handsome figure" in the Hussars' blue and white uniform, caught the eye of the Prince – a man similarly celebrated for his good looks and dress. The Prince, who was thirty-two, befriended the sixteen-year-old Brummell.

In a few short years, Brummell became a captain and made himself the life of the mess hall, but he was an indifferent officer and hardly knew his men. On parade he could only locate his troop because one of the riders had a large red and blue nose. When his nose man transferred to another unit, Brummell mistakenly followed the nose and paraded with the wrong troop. It didn't really matter. Brummell's main objective was not military but social, and he had achieved his victory. He "found himself at once in the highest society in the country."

After he sold his army commission in 1798, Brummell bought a townhouse in London and began his career as the world's first dandy. Prior to Brummell's dandyism, men who were thought to be well dressed were called Macaronis, incroyables, fops, bucks, and beaux. While the different terms implied varying degrees of femininity and sometimes sexual orientation, the men all shared one quality: their dress was showy and complex and featured bright colours and extreme details, including ear-high shirt collars, heavy coat padding, and red heels. Beau Brummell's innovation was that he pulled back from outré details and "affected an extreme neatness and simplicity of dress" which still influences how most men believe other men should dress. Andrew Bolton, curator of the Costume Institute at the Metropolitan Museum, says Brummell "established the contemporary vocabulary for how men dress today. Very sober colours, incredibly tailored garments. . . . They defined the musculature of the male body and even though dandyism later was associated with flamboyance and exhibitionism, and continues to have that association, originally it had a very pared-down aestheticism."

Nineteenth-century prints show Brummell in very fitted riding coats with tails. The coat cuts away to reveal his pelvis and thighs. Brummell wore long pants when knee-length

breeches were still considered the fashion and he was responsible in part for the trend towards ultra-tight pants in the early 1800s. (When it passed, one female fan of Brummellian tightness bemoaned, "At least we always knew what a man was thinking.")

Brummell's opinions were followed avidly by dukes and princes. George, who was now Prince Regent (owing to the mental illness of his father, King George III), would visit Brummell and watch the young dandy go through his ritual of dress, taking note of his habit to carefully tweeze every hair left behind by the razor. If the stories are to believed, the process would take so long, he and the Prince Regent would stay in and dine at home.

As a London fashion critic, Brummell could be at times heedless and aggressive, which is intriguing because in the Regency era insults could lead to duels. Brummell never

BEAU BRUMMELL, WITH A SIMPLE TAILCOAT AND ULTRA-TIGHT PANTS, AVOIDED EXTRANEOUS DETAILS.

cowed anyone with the threat of a duel but he was nevertheless feared. While his quips may sound like mere feints to modern ears, in his time, when context and subtext were everything and social embarrassment keenly felt, Brummell's words could wound deeply. He told one lord he met on the street he thought the noble's shoes were mere slippers. Another time Brummell picked at the lapel of the Duke of Bedford, a close friend, and asked, "Bedford, do you call this thing a coat?"

His reputation for withering remarks grew so large and his opinions held so much sway chaperones would point him out at balls and warn debutantes to make a favourable impression on him or, if they weren't up to the task, to avoid him entirely. One unkind barb from him could ruin a young lady's social prospects.

He did go too far more than once. For some reason, he disliked officers without a noble title moving in his elevated social circle. He once slandered an officer and veteran of the Peninsular War for being "a rank impostor." He said of the man, "I recollect him perfectly, when he was butler at Belvoir [a country estate where Brummell was often a guest]."

He was forced to offer an apology at least once. He was offered five minutes to reply or face consequences. Brummell replied, "In five minutes, sir? In five seconds, or in less time, if you prefer."

It wasn't cowardice, however, that ended his career as an arbiter of fashion. Instead, it was a falling out with the Prince Regent. While there are several versions of what happened between them, the best recounts an incident involving the Bishop of Winchester. After a dinner together, in the presence of the Prince Regent, the bishop pinched some of Brummell's snuff from one of the dandy's fine snuff boxes. Seeing this, Brummell went into a huff and instructed a servant to "throw the rest of the snuff into the fire or on the floor." The Prince Regent, who would one day be the Supreme Governor of the Church of England as George IV, never forgave Brummell for the insult. Later, when Brummell and a companion, Jack Lee, encountered the Prince on the street, the Prince spoke only to Lee, ignoring Brummell. When he went on his way, Brummell asked Lee, loudly enough to be heard, "Who is your fat friend?"

In 1816, Brummell dropped completely from social prominence. Alienated from his royal sponsor, bankrupt, facing the possibility of debtors' prison and with no friend willing to lend him the money he needed, Brummell escaped to Calais and then Caen. There he lived for twenty-four years as a fugitive. Local shopkeepers mockingly referred to him as the King of Calais. And as described by one of Brummell's earliest biographers, William Jesse, Brummell's wardrobe and famous personal hygiene fell into decline as the years passed and he became destitute and lived by begging off his old friends.

One local tailor often offered free services to the dandy when he noticed holes in Brummell's jacket armpits and trousers. "On such occasions," Jesse writes, "poor Brummell was under the necessity of remaining in bed till his trowsers were sent home to him by the friendly tailor, for he had only one pair." He died in 1840.

Brummell's legend continues to grow more than 170 years after his death. Often he is trotted out as a cautionary tale for would-be rakes, but the epitaph for Brummell that appeared in *Harper's Magazine* makes me think of my father: "It has never been advanced that Brummell's heart was bad, in spite of his many faults. Vanity did all. Vanitas vanitatum. O, young men of this age, be warned by a Beau, and flee his doubtful reputation! Peace then to the coat-thinker. Peace to all – to the worst. Let us look within and not judge. It is enough that we are not tried in the same balance."

There are two ways I look at Brummell's career. He was a folk hero, a commoner who told royalty and aristocracy what was what. He also proved that a man of substance and style, a gentleman, can arise from anywhere. The idea had been kicking around for over a century. In 1710, Sir Richard Steele wrote in the *Tatler*, a journal for England's growing middle class, "The courtier, the trader, and the scholar, should all have an equal pretension to the denomination of a gentleman. . . . The appellation of gentleman is never to be affixed to a man's circumstances, but to his behaviour in them." And that's what Brummell did. He rose in social class on his merits, though they were shallow ones: good looks, a sense of style, and an entertaining, though mean-spirited, wit. In the end, Brummell was insufferable. His obsession with correctness ruined the party wherever he went.

WHEN THE KON-TIKI FINALLY CLOSED, MY FATHER was set adrift. He started a number of businesses. He opened a French restaurant called Le Baccarat that tried to evoke the Parisian decadence of the Belle Epoque. In the middle of the dining room, on a raised stage, was a grand piano. The walls were papered in red velvet and the ceiling had gold foil. The restaurant served French onion soup covered in oven-toasted bread and cheese. The menu had a black-and-red drawing of a woman performing the can-can. It was the Moulin Rouge transported to Longueuil, Quebec, a town not known for much beyond having extremely low property values.

My father's sense of style began to change. It was as if entrepreneurship brought out his sleazy side. He started to wear tinted aviator sunglasses and loud printed shirts. He began to hang around a group of men who were apparently his business partners and investors. On the few occasions I had to visit the restaurant, the partners were always sitting on stools at the bar in the closed, airless gloom only night clubs have in the afternoons. Unlike at the Kon-Tiki, there were no offers of ice cream or Jell-O from a jolly chef. My father would count the cash from the night before and split the wad among the men and himself. I knew nothing about restaurant operations, but even I knew what he was doing was wrong. More than the violence and the drinking, my father's dishonesty crushed me. My father was cold-skimming the till. It made keeping the books impossible. The money didn't really belong to him or his partners until the lease, loans, bills, and staff were paid. I felt we no longer owned our lives. Everything we had was borrowed, stolen, ill-gotten, and ready to be taken away. Le Baccarat was bound to fail. Eventually, it did.

My father then started a restaurant consulting business that promised to reverse our fortunes. He opened a small office in Montreal's Chinatown and began designing dining rooms and kitchens for hopeful restaurateurs looking for a quick start-up. He would even build them a set of recipes – always in search of a signature dish – and show them how to create an attractive menu. As part of his research and development, he continued his habit of compulsively stealing menus from other restaurants. Once, he took us kids to a local chophouse. Although we had been there before, this time he noticed they had entirely new menus and pricing. We ate our steak frites without incident, but as we left the restaurant, he reached over the counter, grabbed a menu, and tucked it under his arm like a newspaper. When we got into the car, he tossed the menu onto the passenger side and began to empty his pockets. He pulled out a fork, a table spoon, and a dinner knife. "Look at the nice pattern on the handle," he said.

In the beginning, he was happy being a consultant. He no longer had to spend all his time at a restaurant or conduct business at the bar. He could come home at regular hours and he did. A new weekend ritual developed. Every Saturday morning, we would go shopping at the Champlain Mall. My parents went to Steinberg's with Aimee and Lenny to buy groceries. Tammy would go window shopping for clothes. I would spend the entire time in the toy store Plastica, trying to decide which model airplanes I would lobby my father to buy for me. We would return home for a lunch of Habitant yellow pea soup, a baguette, and creton, a French pork paté.

During this halcyon period, he took me to the air force base in Saint Hubert to watch an air show. My father worked mightily to get me to the front of a line so I could fly in a twin-engine Otter. I was seated in the cabin and a ground crew member in a dull grey jumpsuit helped me fasten the seatbelt. As the plane began to taxi down the runway, my father, sitting behind me, put his hand on my shoulder. It was my first time in an airplane. The engine throttled up and soon we were airborne.

The pilot invited me to sit in the co-pilot seat. I needed little urging. I grabbed the controls, pulling the stick back the way fighter pilots did in the movies. The nose of the plane veered upwards. I could see the underbelly of a helicopter.

"You better let me handle things from here," said the pilot.

When my father and I were back safely on the ground, he said, "Don't tell your mother."

It was the best day ever in a run of good days. The nights could still be bad if he got his hands on a bottle, but the days had become better.

A long career as a consultant could have saved him. It was an outlet for his creativity and mercurial temperament, and allowed him to remain in the food services business, the only business he really knew. More importantly, he was free from the day-to-day grind of running a restaurant and removed from the nightly after-hours wanderings with the restaurant crew.

I wonder now what our life might have been like if he'd been better at collecting payment from his clients. Maybe the good times would have lasted longer, but they didn't. After working hard for three months setting up restaurants for his first batch of clients, he would visit them at their new John Lee–designed eateries with an invoice and good intentions. But instead of coming home to us, he would sit among the empty tables in his clients' empty restaurants and drink with them well into the night. With no money forthcoming, he began accepting barter. One night he came home with an orange ten-speed bicycle to replace my Kamikaze-battered one-speed. Another night it was a blue-faced diving watch. Once, he even came home with a dog. Sheena was a fully trained black Labrador with a small white diamond on her chest. He never bothered to explain why we suddenly had a dog.

But looking back now, I think I finally understand what my father was doing. It wasn't that he was addicted to buying stolen goods at a cheap price, nor was it the thrill of clandestine dealings that made him do it, though that may have been an added attraction for him. It was because he wanted to come home with something to show for his bill-collecting efforts. If he couldn't walk through the door with enough money to pay the mortgage, then he would at least return with a present for his children. They were his tokens of affection.

I CAN'T SHOW BILL – AND DEFINITELY NOT PARK – what I'm doing to my father's suit. Apprentices like me don't get to work on coats whole hog at this stage in the apprenticeship. An apprentice must first learn how to sew, then master attaching buttons, making himself useful quickly. Then he or she must learn to do pockets and lining. Perhaps a sleeve hem or vents can then be done. However, setting a sleeve and cutting, rolling, and finishing a lapel approaches mastery. I am far from ready.

But what am I saying? If you stand back and really consider the situation, I'm not even good enough to be thought of as an apprentice. I'm more of a punchline to a joke, the tailor's apprentice who can't sew. Worse, I'm in hot water. Earlier this week I proposed a revenue-generating scheme. You see, I need the money. As an apprentice I'm not paid a wage, and while I have been writing freelance pieces for various media outlets, I'm not making enough to cover the rent. Like my father, I suppose I was falling into schemes and pipe dreams.

I told Bill I'd found the perfect local factory that could make pants. Not suit pants or odd trousers like flannels, but jeans for people like Nick. It would be worth a try.

"No, no, no," said Bill.

"But think of it, Modernize is nearly a century old. A jean company would kill to have a brand history as old as that."

For Bill, I constructed what fashion designers always refer to as a "story." It's a smidgen of narrative built around a collection so the fashion press can have something to write about. It can get ridiculous. Designers have said in the past they were inspired by Amish minimalism mixed with the cinematic surrealism of David Lynch (Louis Vuitton) or the radical styles of the Black Panthers and Middle Eastern airline hijackers (I'm not joking).

The Modernize story would be more sane. Inspired by the ancient cardboard pant blocks hanging on the nails in the shop. Derived and refined from Victorian pattern-making guides, especially the London trade journal *Tailor and Cutter*, Modernize Tailors jeans would have roots dating all the way back to Vancouver's frontier and resource-town history.

Wasn't it true, I argued, that Modernize made work dungarees for loggers and miners when the shop first opened? We could make hand-finished, even handmade, raw denim jeans and charge twice as much as we charged for dress pants. In fact, I told him, H.D. Lee (rival of Wrangler and Levi's) had reissued back-strap worker's jeans that were selling for up to $300. The timing was perfect.

Bill shook his head.

"Why not? It's a great idea."

"You talk more than you can sew. You should focus on the machine."

He cut me off before I could reply.

"You don't understand," said Bill. "Jeans nearly ruined business for Modernize. When jeans became popular in the Fifties, business dropped and we still haven't recovered from it. Even now, after all these years. But now you're here, you're able to talk to the younger customers, we can be tailors. We can make suits. That's what we do here. No, we'll never do jeans. And you should be focused on learning to sew on the machine."

Bill pointed to the front of the shop and then, for emphasis, patted his flat hand against the top of the cutting table. The motion was gentle but distinctly gavel-like. It let me know it was the end of the discussion.

TAILORS ARE A COLLEGIAL LOT, AND MODERNIZE Tailors is often a clubhouse. Fashion students, wardrobe designers, even a leather jacket maker who makes costumes for a superhero TV show – they all come here to bask in the glow of a genuine operating tailor shop. Semi-retired Persian, South Asian, and Hong Kong immigrant tailors who work out of their basements ostensibly come to our shop to use our ancient buttonhole machine, but a visit is also a break from lonely work.

Dating from the early 1900s, the rig is one of the few in the city able to make keyhole-shaped buttonholes. It is a monstrous machine of black paint and cast iron, with a guillotine blade to cut through wool and large, evil-shaped prongs that look more like harpoons than sewing needles. I'm not allowed to touch it, and I wouldn't dare. I have no idea how to operate it. But it does the job. Bill will put in the buttonholes and the tailors and designers hang around and check out the fabric. Nobody has stock like we do. The conversation never gets too deep but I can tell they get a kick out of the bustle of a crowded workshop. There's nostalgia, there's camaraderie, and while no two tailors make a suit the same way, they can't help but be drawn to one another.

Bill says I should try to be more like David Wilkes. David is seven years younger than I. He is powerfully built and a man who possesses an exceptional amount of grace and good manners. If you imagine breeding a clan of Scotsmen to conquer the world yet rule it benevolently, you would shape them like David. He used to come by the shop in perfectly fitted suits and with a measuring tape draped over his neck, the sign of a true, full-fledged sartorial artist. Bill treats him like a colleague, which, of course, makes me envious. David is also an anomaly; he went to university to learn how to become a tailor.

Raised in Dartmouth, Nova Scotia, David had wanted to be a tailor since the day he visited the Alderney Gate Public Library when he was fourteen. "I found a book that showed me how to hand-sew a buttonhole," says David. It was *The Bantam Step-by-Step Book of Needlecraft* by Judy Brittain. "That was the moment I decided to become a tailor."

Because there were no schools or technical colleges for tailoring, and the tried-and-true tradition of apprenticing to a tailor has fallen into disuse, young David had no way to learn the trade. Even if he had walked up to a shop and offered his fealty to a master tailor, in all likelihood he would have been rejected. Tailoring is greying, and the popularity of Casual Fridays has decreased the demand for tailored clothes. Few tailors can afford to keep an apprentice.

Instead, David enrolled in Dalhousie University's costume design program, offered through the theatre department. In his first six semesters of study, he endured courses in costume history and theatre theory with titles like "The Sculpture of Dress." His ultimate goal was to register in the two-semester tailoring class offered in the fourth year. It was not long enough to teach him all the skills he would need to be a tailor, but it did provide David with a foundation.

After graduating, David found himself again on his own. He was an apprentice without a master, the tailoring equivalent of a ronin, a masterless samurai. He began to amass texts and manuscript facsimiles on the art of tailoring, some of them dating from the early 1700s. Because a great deal of the literature is dedicated to describing methods of pattern-making, David began using his own measurements to create garments based on these formulas. It became his way of travelling through time to experience a wide range of fit and construction. In a way, he made history his teacher and his autodidactic education has served him well.

David used to come in to use our buttonhole machine. Lately though, he hasn't had reason to drop by because he recently purchased a Reece 101 Hand Sewing Buttonhole Machine. He found it online in New York City and had it shipped out to Vancouver.

The Reece now resides in David's bespoke studio, which he runs out of his loft and where he serves a clientele of real estate moguls, best-selling authors, and globe-trotting, Olympics-bound athletes. Luxury retailers turn to him to fix and alter their extremely expensive ready-to-wear items. He is, as Bill has said to me more than once, "the real deal."

Hence my jealousy. But David is also generous with his time, and collegial, which is why I decide to bring my project to him.

This is what progress looks like. David's studio is beautiful. It's on the top floor of a renovated warehouse in a protected heritage district. The windows stretch up to the high ceilings and offer a view of the inlet to the north. Natural light pours in and falls across a giant oak table surrounded by deep leather chairs. A glass case holds some of his ancient tailoring tomes. A true bespoke pink tartan skirt suit waits on a clothes rack for a paying customer. Judging by the cut, the woman has the body of a 1980s supermodel: it's all curves. While both David's studio and Modernize share a quality of clutter – fabric is everywhere – his space is chic and exudes luxury. When I fantasize about becoming a successful tailor, I imagine working in a space just like this.

David pulls out the bolt of pink tartan and offers it to me so I can feel it. The textile is soft, most likely angora tweed. David strokes it too and says, "It's from Paris."

My jacket begins to feel tawdry in my hands. I show it to him anyway. He sees how I attempted to use a straight stitcher at home to close the edge of the lapel. The stitches wavered left and right, an inebriated line, and formed unsightly dimples along the edge. Then I tried again by hand but the back-stitches are unevenly spaced. David takes the jacket and inspects my handiwork. "They're fine, they're fine. Most people wouldn't notice it." He is being gracious.

He asks, "Do you know how to do a ladder stitch?" When I tell him no, he rummages through his workbench and pulls out a suitable scrap. He licks a thread and puts it through the eye of a needle. "I picked this up years ago," he says and begins to sew a seam. The thread goes in and out of the cloth but he makes no back-stitches nor does he create any loops. At first it looks like a rudimentary running stitch, but then he pulls at the end of the thread and the stitches disappear into the seam, becoming invisible.

One can read a hundred technical guides or follow countless online how-to videos, but nothing compares to the passing on of a skill from one person to another face to face. To acquire real know-how, you have to see it with your own eyes, the raw, unabridged step by step. Not only do you see the necessary sequence, but you also see how a person stands or moves, you get a feel for the body English needed to do something well. You get a sense of which parts of the task are difficult and which are easy. You can feel the shift in balance and which muscles are needed. Sometimes you just need a person to spend fifteen minutes with you to teach you how to do something right. This is what lies at the heart of an apprenticeship. When David hands me the sample and makes me promise to try the stitch at home, I feel I've become a new link in a chain of knowledge. Maybe one day I too will show an apprentice the ladder stitch.

Next, David wants to show me his Reece. The machine is painted in what I think of as institutional green – the colour of school lockers, drill presses, and hospital walls – but it is, nevertheless, a fine piece of technology. The Reece is a fetish object among tailors in the same way that a Leica rangefinder camera can make photography buffs salivate. A functioning Reece of any age can easily cost more than $2,700. What makes it so desirable is its ability to create a keyhole buttonhole; that is, a buttonhole wider at one end. It also finishes the edges more cleanly than an expert tailor would by hand. In fact, it is an even finer machine than the one we have at Modernize. It is a triumph of invention and persistence.

Beginning in the 1700s, would-be inventors of sewing, embroidery, and buttonhole machines attempted to create contraptions just like the Reece, which would emulate the kinds of stitches done by hand. It was a quest that led many down a long, frustrating path to nowhere. Take the running stitch, for example. It is among the simplest in the repertoire of hand-sewing. The needle goes in and comes out at a different point, then repeat. It is so easy, even a very young child can do it. But could a machine?

The first sewing machine patent was issued to Charles Weisenthal in 1755. In theory Weisenthal's machine should have produced the running stitch. The patent showed the needle was to be threaded through the middle. A topside armature made the needle pierce the fabric and then a second arm grabbed the needle on the other side of the fabric. The fabric would advance and then the second arm would move up and pierce the fabric, handing the needle back to the first arm. But this invention existed only on paper. No functioning prototype was ever produced by Weisenthal. The technology of the eighteenth and early nineteenth centuries was simply too crude to mimic human movement.

The breakthrough came when designers abandoned the idea of passing the needle completely through the fabric. Instead, they envisaged prototypes built around the concept of having needles controlled by armatures on only one side. On the other side, thread would have to catch the needle by hook or entanglement. Clearly, mechanical timing was an essential ingredient for the early machine's success. Historical timing helped too. Barthélemy Thimonnier had one but not the other.

Described as "a dissolute young tailor of St. Etienne, who did not like plying the needle himself," Thimonnier patented wooden machines with a crochet needle that could pull a thread up from under, form a loop on top, and, with the next drive of the needle, anchor the first loop with the second loop, forming a chain stitch. It worked well enough to go into production. In 1831, he had eighty machines sewing army uniforms. Unfortunately for Thimonnier, the machines were viewed as a threat by tailors and seamstresses. Some accounts say the atelier suffered ongoing sabotage. All agree a mob of two hundred needle-trade workers ransacked his factory, throwing pieces of the machines through the windows. Thimonnier was forced to flee for his life from the burning factory.

The unlucky tailor-cum-inventor escaped carrying a lone surviving chain-stitcher on his back. Losing nearly everything in the fire, a destitute Thimonnier "kept soul and body together by exhibiting its performance as a curiosity." He refused to give up on his invention. In 1845, he improved the design, enabling the machine to make two hundred stitches per minute. With the backing of a manufacturer, Thimonnier's latest model was ready to change the course of tailoring. By 1848, he had set up a new workshop and again a mob descended upon his machines. Thimonnier never recovered. For thirty years, he struggled to find a place for his invention, the right backer, another chance.

No one gave it to him. Thimonnier died in poverty at the age of sixty-four, his dream unfulfilled.

Thimonnier nevertheless established the template. His legacy is everywhere. Now, it is nearly unfathomable to have any significant hand-stitching on factory-made clothes. There are machines with scythe-like curved needles able to sew plain, uncuffed pant hems with invisible stitching using clear nylon thread. There are machines able to align and negotiate the four holes of a button and make cross-stitches over the fasteners in the same way a tailor would by hand. There are even devices capable of making the running stitch using Weisenthal's concept of passing a needle between two arms.

Having access to such wondrous machines of the kind only dreamed of by early inventors can present a tailor with a quandary. As machines aid in the tailor's art, they can also impede it. Machines can, unless one is willing to go to Thimonnier's back-breaking effort of lugging one around, take away a tailor's mobility and self-reliance.

Even in an age of computer-aided cutting machines and heavy-duty walking foot, clutch-driven, puller-feed, double-needle chain stitchers, a tailor needs few tools. Rory Duffy called me recently to tell me he had moved to New York. He had just gotten married to a woman who was an executive with a major American fashion label and was now waiting to set up his own shop. Until then, he was still making suits for Londoners from tiny bundles of wool sent to him by cutters (though the great houses prefer to have their tailors on the premises and, like an errant prince, Duffy may one day be recalled). I asked him about his set-up. He told me he was

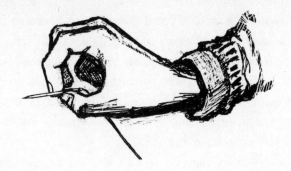

sewing out of the den with a domestic iron and ironing board, his own scissors, and a few bobbins of thread and needles. "That's all you really need."

It's true. Another tailor I know is Renzo Montagliani, a seventy-five-year-old who runs a shop in the old Italian area of Vancouver called The Drive. Like Bill, he is from the old school. Renzo started tailoring at eleven to escape life as a priest in Italy. He immigrated to Canada after the Second World War and ran his first neighbourhood tailoring business with his brother Romeo before striking out on his own a few years later. He has spent the last five decades in the same corner storefront boutique. From his shop window, he has seen the march of time go by. Hippies and, later, yuppies moved into the area, bringing with them organic food shops and co-op bookstores but little need for suits. Nevertheless, he got by with a steady stream of politicians, Canadian football quarterbacks, and movie stars coming through. If you wanted to make a mark in this city, at some point you would get a suit from Renzo. But those days have faded and Renzo confesses to me he is too old to ride the new wave of interest in suits. He aims to retire. And, with apologies to Rory Duffy and David Wilkes, when an old tailor hangs up his scissors a light goes out in the sartorial firmament, a star disappears. Everything he knows about suits – Italian-fit suits with narrow shoulders, tight waists, and pants "that are gonna fit perfect," by which he means tight and tapered ("That's Italian," Renzo says) – will be trapped, left inert, in his hands.

Renzo shows them to me. He tells me his fingers have begun cramping and in the morning they're sore. He just went through triple bypass surgery. Unlike Bill, he is truly ready to retire. "It'll be hard to do but that's my life."

But, he says, on the brighter side, he has big plans to travel. Then he tells me about his last trip to Morocco. He and his wife were winding their way through the narrow lanes of Marrakech when they stumbled upon a tailor's shop. In Morocco, like many places in the developing world, a tailor has no more gear than Rory does. Tables, irons, even lights are not necessary. A tailor can simply sit on the stoop of his windowless shop. A foot-powered treadle straight-stitching machine (just as likely to be a Singer as an Usha or a Shiv) is nice but not essential. This shop was no different, and Renzo introduced himself to the tailor with a looping hand gesture that could not be mistaken for anything but an overcast stitch to indicate his profession. Before Renzo's wife knew it, Renzo had made himself at home hand-sewing buttons with his Moroccan colleagues.

It isn't just about being able to find a job anywhere in the world. It's about spanning distance, race, history, time. The tailor's craft is old, maybe even dying, and yet the thought of Renzo sitting beside his new friends speaks to something human, universal, and eternal – at least to tailors.

Maybe tailors are becoming obsolete because what they make can't be made obsolete. Tailors provide handmade or, at the very least, personally-made suits that can last forever. They labour in a world where quickly produced throwaway fashion makes today's looks already passé. Profit is made through churn and burn, wear it, trash it, then shop again. A tailor-made suit isn't like that. It can last a lifetime and then some, to the perplexity of sons everywhere. There are thousands, perhaps millions of suits in young men's closets, waiting again for a tailor's touch to reconcile, when possible, the trace of the father to the body of the son. And then there is the touch, the over-familiar yet comforting hand that pats down the shoulders and smoothes the back when a man puts on his altered suit for the first time. The soothing contact slips and melds into the reverie: I am wearing my father's suit. And the customer may not know it, but the tailor touches him in a doting, gentle manner he may not have felt since childhood.

So, there is a trade-off. Machines are faster. They provide straighter lines, even arguably better stitches, and cause less eye strain. But hand-sewing is internalized. It is tactile. It leaves behind a fingerprint. There is no whirring of electric motors or tug of metal gears feeding fabric into the kill-zone of a plunging needle. There is only the circle made by a tailor's hand as he quietly pulls the thread that connects all the parts together.

Unless your family has its own coat of arms or you are entitled to wear a distinguished club button, the classiest choice is the plain, flat, English gilt button with a shank that must be anchored into the cloth.

Alan Flusser, *Dressing the Man* (2002)

MY FATHER'S BRASS BUTTONS HAVE NO LOGOS OR pseudo-heraldry adorning them. They have a quiet basket weave or checkerboard pattern. The raised squares on the top button on the front have been polished to golden by my father's fingers and thumb working the fastener through the buttonhole. In its recesses, a dark patina of grime has collected. The other buttons are uniformly dull. They have hardly been handled, which is no surprise. Like all suits, my father's jacket has an excess of buttons serving no real purpose. For example, the bottom button on my father's two-button blazer serves no use at all, since two-button coats follow the Always-Never rule. Then on each sleeve dangle three more buttons, which are anchored at the sleeve ends by their shanks. They have no corresponding buttonholes and, as far as I can tell, do nothing, except smell like old pennies.

Blazer buttons follow their own code. They can bear the mark or insignia of an organization, or a group, even a military unit. If you wear the button you are saying you are one of them. In England and establishment burgs like Boston or New York, it is considered in poor taste to sport nonsensical symbols. But worse is appropriating one that does not belong to you. For example, if you choose to wear a button depicting an eagle grasping an anchor, you might one day be approached by a man with gigantic arms and a tattoo. You may notice he has no legs and has wheeled up to you in a wheelchair. He will ask you, "Where did you serve?" And you will say, "Pardon me?" And he will say to you again, "Where did you serve?" and he will point to your buttons, saying, "These are U.S. Marine Corps buttons." Then he will spin around and begin to roll away, but between propulsions of his piston-like arms he will salute you with one finger. *Semper fi.*

The origins of the blazer and its flashy buttons are again to be found in the Victorian era. In 1837, if the legend is to be believed, the newly crowned Queen Victoria visited Her Majesty's steam vessel *Blazer*, a Tartarus-class wood-paddle sloop with five guns and a 136-horsepower steam engine. At the time, the Royal Navy had no formal uniform for seamen. Commanders had autonomy regarding on-board attire, and one captain of the *Harlequin* became infamous for making his crew dress like, well, harlequins. To the great benefit of the evolution of menswear, the commander of the *Blazer*, Lieutenant John Middleton Waugh, had other designs. To sharpen the crew's appearance for the young Queen, he ordered double-breasted blue serge jackets.

Some accounts say the buttons were brass, others suggest they were black. Regardless of the colour, for good measure, the commander had tailors sew more buttons onto the sailors' sleeves to prevent the crew from wiping their noses on their new clothes. The story goes that the Queen was so taken by the appearance of the men of the *Blazer* she subsequently made the blue jackets the standard uniform for the Royal Navy. The story may be no more than a tall tale but it is nevertheless a good one.

An alternate origin story can be found in *Dickens's Dictionary of Oxford and Cambridge*, edited by Charles Dickens, which defines the blazer as a "flannel jacket, worn by a member of any of the Athletic Clubs, of the proper Club colours. . . . The name was probably first given to the scarlet jacket of the Lady Margaret Boat Club." The Lady Margaret members certainly blazed in scarlet, but they were not the only ones wearing flamboyant jackets. Perusing through the brackets of boat races among Cambridge clubs in the 1880s, one can't help but admire the riot of colours. Blazers were striped, piped, and ribboned, rivalling the foppery of the Court of King Charles II. For example, a rower of the Jesus College Boat Club wears a "white straw hat with red and black ribbon, white blazer trimmed with red and black, jersey trimmed with red and black, red and black socks." Pembroke College Boat Club can be recognized by its "dark blue blazer trimmed with light blue ribbon, red martlet on pocket, white jersey trimmed with light and dark blue, white straw hat trimmed with light and dark blue." Another team of eight wears black and yellow. It is cerise with white silk for the Corpus Christi Club.

I am describing the arcane to you. Only a very select few will ever have the privilege to access exclusive yacht or rowing clubs with their own secret symbols. But who can resist the blazer with its glittering buttons?

Would I be an impostor if I found a mark to fill the face of the buttons on my father's suit? What design would best represent my father and me? What would say we once belonged to each other? A pair of eyeglasses would be a nice choice. I rarely saw him without his glasses on and disliked it when he didn't wear them. In fact, it frightened me. He looked too young. How could such a young man be my father? And without his glasses, his face became downcast. No, I liked him better with his glasses on. His frames braced his face into a more stoic countenance.

Perhaps the little man from the Johnny Walker bottle would make a good symbol, at least for my father. He always seemed to have a bottle of Scotch around. He enjoyed cognac, wine, and beer, but Scotch was his talismanic drink. I used to ask him why he drank it. He always said he enjoyed it for the taste and not the alcohol. He would drink it at work at the end of a shift. Then on the way home he would find a place to take another drink. When he got home he would often drink more from a heavy crystal tumbler cut with a knobbly geometric pattern, maybe because it offered a better grip.

My father and I did belong to a fraternity group once. It was the Lee's Benevolent Association of Montreal. Its members comprised Lees from the same village as my father. Everyone acted as if they were my uncles, but I didn't know how I was related to them, if at all, and I still don't. Nor do

I have any clue to whom they were benevolent. Every year, my father would drag me to their annual banquet. Perhaps my father was required to put his first son on display. All I really knew was every year we would be served tripe, crispy chicken, and shark fin soup at the Kam Fung restaurant in Montreal's Chinatown. At the centre of the table, next to a bucket of ice, would be a bottle of Coke, 7-Up, and Johnny Walker Red.

The last time I attended the banquet was in 1983. I was thirteen and in grade eight at Chambly County High School. I had just discovered punk and New Wave pop music. Before then it was Cheap Trick, Kiss, Journey, and Styx. But now there was also Pat Benatar, the Human League, Joan Jett and the Blackhearts, ABC, and Roxy Music (Bryan Ferry in a white tuxedo jacket! Bryan Ferry in a leather jacket *and* a black bow tie!).

I was an emergent teen taking a serious interest in my appearance. Clothes had become Fashion instead of simply playing dress-up. I experimented with turning my hair into a vertical spray. I wore pale Lois jeans for girls with yellow top-stitching. My style ambitions were tentative and contingent. One day I would wear jeans torn to shreds, the next I would put on a white cotton blazer (where did I find it?) and would sashay to the school bus with the song "Avalon" playing in my head. Most days I wore what my mother bought me – rugby pants and tennis shirts – but the seeds of my sartorial sensibility were there.

I would borrow my father's dress shirts and wear them rolled up at the sleeves and hanging loose over my pants. It was a thrill to wear them. I felt like an alchemist. The clothes transformed me, made me grown-up. I in turn changed the clothes: what looked all business on my father became romantic, dissolute, and worldly on me.

That night I wore one of my father's shirts with a pair of black pointy oxford lace-ups. My pants were black-on-black cotton seersucker, and woven in such a way that they were both ribbed and puckered. The legs had originally ballooned out and swung about loosely, but perhaps because I had seen a certain New Wave video, I had recently sewn up the calves tight. The pants now looked like jodhpurs. I felt very dressed up.

Nevertheless, the dinner was, as usual, a mortifying drag. I hardly spoke any Cantonese, though I understood enough to know that what the old men of the association were saying about me was bad.

"He doesn't speak Chinese?"

"Why doesn't he speak Chinese?"

"You should have taught him."

"He's a ghost face."

"He's English. He's juk sing, like a cup with no opening, he is unfulfilled."

"He's not really Chinese."

At the time my father was still a young man. If I met him on the street now as he was then, I would find him callow, loud-mouthed, and insecure. He was still growing into his manhood and without certain defences. He was often mistaken for being a much younger man, even a teen, as I had at that age. The haranguing by the old men of the association must have left him feeling emasculated. To the elders, my father was a mystery. What was the use of carrying on a bloodline without passing on a language and a culture? To them, it was another unbelievably grand twist in the failed dream of *Gum San*, Gold Mountain. Canada. At our table, I was the joke of the evening, or at least it felt that way. I took refuge in eating. My father sank deeper into his glass. He might have started with an ounce of Scotch and a mountain of ice, but as the evening progressed his glass became more amber, as it filled with more Scotch and less ice. He slumped into a miserable silence.

By the end of the night things boiled over. We were walking back to the car when the only woman in attendance caught up with us. She was an old crone, possibly an esteemed matriarch of some distant branch of the family, who wielded the evil eye like a throwing star. She wagged her crooked finger up and down at what I was wearing. She barked at my father, wagged her finger some more, then stomped off.

"What was she saying?"

My father's face fell and then turned red.

"She says you're dressed like a waiter."

It was my first acute awareness that my father could be ashamed of me. I tucked in my shirt and rolled down my sleeves. My pants and the purple belt I wore to hold them up now seemed ridiculous, clownish. My father looked at me as he finished his cigarette.

"You look like a bum," he said, and then he flicked the butt into the gutter.

On the drive home from the banquet, I couldn't muster indignation or anger. It wasn't that my emotions were muted. No, everything was keenly felt. We didn't speak to each other at all on the way home.

Driving through Old Montreal, we passed a series of old factories and the grain silos at the docks standing like dimly lit silent monoliths. To escape Montreal and head back home we had to cross the Victoria Bridge. The span was decked with steel grating and our tires droned with unearthly overtones punctuated by rhythmic clunks every time we hit a seam. As we turned right to merge onto the highway by the Saint Lawrence River, I remembered how we used to play a game on nights like this, when he was sober and we were in the front of the car together. We would pretend the car was the USS *Enterprise* of Starfleet. He was the helmsman. I was in charge of the weapons. We would both give out commands. He would let me push the glowing buttons for the radio and the air conditioning, unleashing a full spread of photon torpedoes that would annihilate the cars in front of us, and then my father would punch the car into warp drive and we would speed down the straightaway before we reached our exit. We were both too old to play it, but it was still our game.

That night, though, I just looked out my window. I watched the river and the searchlight on Place Ville Marie tower, which would fan across the sky as a beacon and warning for airplanes descending to Dorval Airport. I could see the giant illuminated cross sitting atop Mount Royal, rising up from the heart of Montreal Island. He continued to drive in silence. The things that were important between us were slipping by and neither of us knew how to hold onto them.

I pretended to sleep. The buttons remained untouched. Only the sound of the road filled the distance.

When I got ready for school the next morning, I didn't bother borrowing a shirt.

IN THE CURRENT CULTURE OF FAST FASHION, WHERE a certain designer look can hit the runway in Milan and then be knocked-off and available for sale in a cheap chic retail chain in a matter of weeks, it's hard to believe there are enduring ideas in the garment trade. But in wearing the modern suit – stripped of the embroidery, embellishment, and florid colours that first fell out of vogue during the French Revolution (in France at least, such baroque details and stylings were associated with the discredited aristocracy) – men continue to dress, however inadvertently, in a manner that owes much to the neoclassical revivalists. Across Europe, these were men and women of the late eighteenth and early nineteenth centuries who believed Ancient Greek architecture and art could not be surpassed. As one English philhellenist wrote in 1814, "The remnants of the Greek architecture still afford models, which, never having been equalled, seem incapable of being further improved."

Neoclassicism reached a sustained peak with the arrival of the Elgin Marbles in England in 1806. The collection included some of the best sculptural works of Phidias taken from the Parthenon Temple in the Acropolis. (After much squabbling about whether the removal of the antiquities from Greece constituted cultural pillaging, they were eventually installed in the British Museum.) The sculptures created a sensation. Lord Byron condemned their removal from Athens in his poem "The Curse of Minerva." John Keats was so taken with them he wrote two sonnets, both dwelling on the nature of mortality and what it means to create something that transcends the ages.

Tailors and the fashion press couldn't help but be influenced by the belief that the ancient Greek forms on display at the museum were perfect and therefore, by inference, should provide a model for their tailoring. The cutters and tailors of London flocked to the museum to take note of the heroic forms and proportions of the classical figures, but this presented them with a puzzle. If the naked male form as portrayed in these statues was indeed perfect, how could tailors improve upon the perfect "naked state"? In *The Gazette of Fashion*, one writer put the dilemma this way: "How would they clothe such perfection?"

Tailors had to rethink their methods of measuring, proportion, pattern cutting, padding, and sewing to eliminate the once acceptable wrinkles and draping found in male fashion of the previous centuries and come up with a garment that would imitate the smoothness of sculpted marble. They were after the next best thing to being nude. To wit: they simplified the suit. Blame Brummell or Phidias, but all the extraneous details – the ruffles, gathers, billows, and ribbons – were left off. The range of colours was winnowed and a narrower, darker palette favoured. All in the pursuit of a sleek and homogenous masculine surface.

Broad shoulders, a waspish waist, and long striding legs: the suit was devolving to the heroic first principles of plate armour. The new modern nineteenth-century man was to be clad in, as Anne Hollander put it to me, "his honesty and his integrity, 'in native worth and honour clad,' meaning naked. That's from Milton. A suit is supposed to suggest that underneath there is Adam, innocent and pure, and also Apollo, full of creative zeal and energy and total balance and beauty in all directions, and infinitely sexually attractive to everybody, of every sex."

It still holds true. The modern tailor remains under the sway of neoclassicism. Even if he has never set eyes on an ancient Greek sculpture or pored over centuries of studies to crack the secret code of the body's most beautiful and classical proportions, a tailor will work to enhance a client's figure and help the suit-wearing man achieve those divine proportions. One need not look very far to appreciate the currency of the two-thousand-year-old aesthetic: superhero comic books and *America's Next Top Model* abound with such classical forms.

It isn't simply about being tall and leggy. The proportions have always been mathematically precise and were first set down by Vitruvius, the Roman architect and ardent admirer of Greek art. In the first century BCE, Vitruvius outlined the human body's most handsome proportions in his treatise *The Ten Books of Architecture*. Vitruvius believed architectural

[149]

columns should share proportions that related to the ideal human form. The figure of the Vitruvian Man, as we now call him, has ideal proportions as determined by an elaborate system. His face is one-tenth the height of his entire body. His shoulders are one-quarter as wide as he is tall. His torso is three heads tall, his legs four heads tall, and so on. Painters, sculptors, architects, and scientists believed the Vitruvian Man's proportions corresponded perfectly to the ear-pleasing harmonies of the thirds, fourths, and fifths found in music. And this relationship proved there was a universal set of ratios found in nature that were inherently beautiful. Things made according to these ratios would appear as "music to the eye."

The most famous illustration of Vitruvian Man comes from the quill of Leonardo da Vinci. Leonardo's drawing shows a man with his arms and legs extended within a circle and square. While some artists depicted Vitruvian Man with a sterile bald head, Leonardo's version has curly locks and a curious scowl, the precursor to Derek Zoolander's Blue Steel. Perhaps it is a flattering self-portrait. Most assuredly, this Vitruvian Man would look wonderful in a suit. A tight one-button with a short jacket hem, no vent, and pants cuffed at the bottom would provide the right amount of Italian sophistication. This man would require very little padding.

But as Hollander explains, the suit, especially the jacket, became a garment that could support padding. As a result, even those who were considered disproportionate by tailors could have the bodies of Achilles or Alexander or, in our time, Superman. Tailors learned to create athletic and warrior bodies, and they strove to make suits look good in movement.

(Remember, the figures depicted in the Elgin Marbles are in battle.) As a result, throughout the nineteenth century numerous pattern and cutting systems were created to help tailors draft sleeves, shoulders, and collars that wouldn't bunch or lift or gape. Movement was built into the cut of a coat. It still is. An empty suit jacket does not lie flat if thrown on the bed. It has a liveliness. The sleeves go akimbo and the shoulders will roll up as if the coat were trying to sit up.

As Hollander says, the suit is made for action: "You can look good in a suit no matter what figure you've got. And this is the point. Along with that padding comes a certain harmony with the way the whole thing overlaps. James Bond used to do this: climb into a submarine and come out of it on land, shake yourself, and you're ready for the diplomatic reception without a moment's pause or a look in the mirror. That's the way the suit becomes a modern, advanced, mobile object. It does everything. It is utilitarian. But mainly, it keeps your physical self like that of a panther or a gazelle, ready to go anywhere in its beautiful coat."

With a suit the wearer is both naked and dressed, animal and human. In a suit a man is made whole (with the most divine of all ratios: one to one) in a way no other garment can.

THERE ARE AFTERNOONS WHEN MY FATHER AND I still lie together on the couch. I put my palm to his and measure my hand against his. My father bends his fingers and mine bow back until I have to pull them away. I make him curl his leg up so I can also compare our feet. Heels aligned, my big toe barely reaches the balls of his hot, dry feet.

"Hey," he says. "Get up. Make a fist."

I sit up and clench my hands. He grabs my wrists and untucks my thumbs from beneath my fingers and wraps them over my knuckles.

"You'll break your thumbs if you hit someone like that," he explains. "Now punch me."

I wind up and hit his palm as hard as I can. He sits up now and plants his feet. He takes me by the shoulders and shuffles me over so I'm square in front of him. He holds up a palm. "Punch me again."

I wind up and poke at his right hand. "No," he says. "Don't

raise your shoulder. You have no power when you do that. Keep your shoulder down and don't bend your wrists."

He draws a line with his finger from my index and middle knuckles up along my forearms to my shoulders. All of this, he tells me, should be one. "With these two knuckles, punch me again." He offers his deltoid muscle as a target.

I hit him. He tells me to rotate my forearm as I punch so my thumb points downwards when I land the blow. He wants me to shift my weight. I strike him again. He staggers just a little but I'm encouraged.

"Now, I want you to punch through me. Make the energy go through me. Don't stop where I am but go past me. Do you understand?"

I don't understand but I jab him harder. His shoulder muscle feels like a smooth round rock able to bear, it seems, any blow, any weight.

⚸

I am holding a folding knife over my father's suit and getting ready to cut into the shoulders. Not through the fabric, but along the seams between the sleeve head and the body. I find myself thinking about what my father was trying to teach me that day more than thirty years ago, as he showed me how to fight in the basement. What was the grand project he was working on? What final result was he after?

Cutting the lapels was hard, but slicing into the shoulders is harder. I'm using an unorthodox technique and incising or, rather, I am scraping with the blade, working my way into the seam, probing tentatively through three rows of hard waxy stitches. I am doing my best not to slice the wool. One slip will mean the end of the suit.

Even experienced tailors have anxieties about working the shoulders of a suit. Again, it comes down to geometry. The shoulders make a barrel-vault shape capping the larger tube of the torso, and the sleeves are thinner tubes that must be inserted into the larger tube. But there's more to it. The sleeves are not perpendicular to the body but parallel to it, and the tailor must create a sleeve head that redirects the sleeve ninety degrees into the armhole of the body without unsightly gathers, creases, or divots. In addition, each man's arms drop down at a particular angle. In my case, if my arms were minute hands, I would say they hang forward at around twenty-six minutes in a slightly simian slouch. If the sleeves don't match the natural fall of a man's arms, the sleeves will pull too far forward or back and become another source of wrinkles across the upper arms.

Simply put, having a novice like me detach and reset a sleeve is asking for trouble.

But I have to go in. I don't have my father's shoulders and never will. I have to narrow the blazer's shoulders by an inch and a half on each side. To avoid the risk of changing the sleeve angle, I will detach only the top of the armhole, leaving the armpit to remain safely affixed.

I've burrowed the blade deep enough into the seam to begin cutting the threads, which offer the same meaty resistance as when I slide a knife through the joint of a chicken thigh. Inside I find more of the alarming spewing guts of the suit: thin wafers of synthetic material are stacked to make the shoulder pad. The foamy stuff seems to be heated strands of polyethylene or polypropylene blown into a spongy texture, like the white stuffing you find in a cheap Ikea couch. The shoulders are reinforced by a stiff burlap-like lining glued to the wool to help give the armhole shape.

I don't like all the padding. It's the reason why the suit hovers off my body – my main discomfort with the suit. It inflates the jacket and gives my upper body a bloated and pompous shape. I understand the point of padding, but in the case of my father's suit it's not working.

Ready-to-wear suits like my father's are pumped out of factories according to a sizing chart and a predetermined set of dimensions. But even though I might be a size 36 chest, I'm not like all the other size-36-chest men in the world. Yet I'm being asked to live with the fit, and with the padding added on top. A ready-to-wear suit can make the wearer feel like he is the problem. But, I'm not. The suit is the problem.

I wish my father's suit were as easy and effortless to wear as a T-shirt. I like T-shirts because they are very matter-of-fact: there is no lining or canvas. There isn't much difference between how my not-quite-Apollonian body looks when naked and how my body looks in a T-shirt. There are no surprises or disappointments. With a T-shirt, body and cloth are one and the same. The T-shirt simply wraps around you. It's a plain, honest article of clothing, which, when one thinks about it, was the original point of the suit.

A great-fitting tee can also be had cheaply. You rip it out of the plastic bag and you put it on. What's not to like?

Okay, I avoid printed T-shirts, but if you told me I could wear only plain T-shirts for a year, I'd have no problem. With the right blazers, sports coats, and pants, I could make it work. A T-shirt could even be worn for a creative black tie. (An Alexander Wang scoop neck in semi-shiny Tencel would do just the trick for an evening out.)

The T-shirt became acceptable outerwear in 1951 thanks to Marlon Brando. Before Brando, the T-shirt was considered underwear and not thought of as proper dress for the city or school campus. Day labourers and sharecroppers may have worn them openly on the job, but even during the height of the Depression they would put on a denim or chambray shirt before allowing themselves to be photographed. Then Brando wore a T-shirt for his iconic role as the working-class brute Stanley Kowalski in the film *A Streetcar Named Desire*, and the craze for T-shirts began.

The inspiration to have Brando wear a T-shirt both in the original 1947 production of the play and in the film version came from the actor himself. He would show up at rehearsal wearing one and director Elia Kazan could not overlook his insouciant snub of dress etiquette. It was perfect for Kowalski.

Brando's appearance however was not merely an extension of his Method acting technique. He was a real culture rebel who wore T-shirts off-stage and off-screen and shared his character's disregard for propriety. Kazan said of Brando's appearance at rehearsal, "Marlon looked like the shit had been beaten out of him . . . which it probably had. All the cast knew that Marlon was fucking every woman in sight and, for a change of pace, picking up rough trade along the waterfront."

Either way, Kazan needed Brando in the provocative T-shirt. With the help of costume designer Lucinda Ballard, Brando further obliged by wearing tight jeans. Brando insisted on not wearing underwear during fittings because he wanted his jeans to fit like a "second skin." Ballard tapered his jeans to showcase his genitals and tightened the top as well so his muscles bulged beneath the jersey material.

While Brando was not the first person to wear a T-shirt with a pair of jeans, he was the one who elevated the rebel attire to iconic fashion items. Brando's rebel influence was felt even at Modernize. In the 1950s, fewer teen boys came into the shop for their first suit. However, the shop then became the place in Vancouver to get strides and drapes, high-waisted baggy pants associated with youth gangs. In fact, drapes became 95 percent of Bill and Jack's business.

Can a suit ever beat the fit and comfort of a T-shirt? Tailors and fashion designers have tried. In the 1960s, London experienced the Peacock Revolution, a counter-cultural movement that celebrated androgyny and brought back the ruffles, ribbons, and embroidery not popular in menswear since before the French Revolution. Suits became tighter and lighter, especially those found in ready-to-wear boutiques. Unhindered by the history and tradition of Savile Row, manufacturers felt free to adopt tailoring techniques from Italy, where the warmer climate called for suits with less interfacing, softer lines, and lighter fabrics. But the suits still didn't feel like a T-shirt.

Then Giorgio Armani burst onto the scene with his first collection in 1975. He introduced the unconstructed sports coat. (Later, he would define the power suit proportions of the 1980s, the trend which influenced the design of my father's suit, but here we are speaking of very early Armani.) These had a minimum of padding in the body and were often half-lined. And though the shoulders were broad, Armani's suits softened the masculine silhouette. The fabric draped. Some argued the suits were baggy, though, admittedly, in an expressive way. Armani suits were attractive and comfortable.

Echoing the rise of the T-shirt, Armani's take on the coat vaulted into mainstream consciousness by way of another film, *American Gigolo,* and another smouldering movie idol. As aptly put by Constance White in the *New York Times,* "In the 1980 film, Richard Gere surveyed his wardrobe of pale suits, earth-tone jackets and genteel striped shirts, and in the span of a movie telegraphed two words to any male viewer who ever craved sexual power: Giorgio Armani."

Armani became "King of the Blazer" in America. He showed the suit need not speak only of an Apollonian body of perfection. There could be a looser, even coarser, form of masculinity, one that, unlike the Peacock Revolution, did not have to indulge in androgyny. Armanis had swagger. In 1982, the designer made the cover of *Time* magazine and the ensuing decade saw fashion become obsessed with shoulders: big shoulders, sagging shoulders. They became as one designer noted the "antithesis of Savile Row." They made a suit look like "a hand-me-down." Another said they made a suit "less English, more hip."

The unconstructed jacket and its offspring in subsequent collections troubled traditional tailors. Interfacing, linings, padding, the hidden handmade yet essential elements of a suit – these were what had always separated the well from

the cheaply made. Now, the underpinnings of a good suit were becoming devalued, even irrelevant.

Bill tells me that when Armanis first came into the shop for alterations in the early 1980s, they were curiosities. They were made more like a dress shirt than a jacket. Neither Bill nor Park had any interest in copying them per se. Tailors are notorious for making suits their own way in a house style, and some take great pride in not caring how others make their suits. Nevertheless, the Armanis did present a puzzle. How did they keep their shape? Why did they have such a fine drape? What attracted men to this type of off-the-rack jacket as opposed to what Modernize could offer – custom and made-to-measure, the perfect fit? Bill may never have deigned to stoop low enough to emulate an Armani, but when a sample came through the shop he did poke around

HIS LOOSE, SWAGGERING, LOW-BUTTON STANCES AND NOTCHES MADE GIORGIO ARMANI THE "KING OF BLAZERS."

the innards to see what was going on. The tailors at Modernize were not alone.

In 1990, the sewing magazine *Threads* trumpeted its dissection of an Armani jacket as if it were a tell-all exposé, breathlessly promising to reveal "the secrets of the Master of Milan." *Threads* writer Anne Hyde found in her sample cleverly placed fusibles (yes, iron-on synthetics). She could see how the fabric fell from the shoulders and relied on the designer's talent for inventive pattern making. Armani put seams where no traditional tailor ever would. For example, he placed a seam at the back of the jacket collar, which made it easier for the collar to lie flat. Traditional tailors achieved the same effect on a one-piece collar through fire, water, iron, and wood: they used steam, pressure, and battery with clappers to force flat wool to curl around the neck. Armani's fabrics also impressed Hyde. They were of unsurpassed quality and were the designer's secret ingredient. They gave the coat shape and body. But what Hyde and tailors like Bill could not detect by unravelling Armani's clothes was the designer's overarching desire for freedom.

Born in Italy before the Second World War, Armani remembered midnight retreats into bomb shelters and playing amidst blasted ruins. He was nearly blinded when he and his friends threw a bag of explosives on a fire. Often, he and his family went hungry. After the war, Armani recalled making tearful prison visits to see his father, who was incarcerated for being a fascist sympathizer. Is it any surprise then that his innovation, as fashion writer Suzie Mackenzie concludes, came out of a "desire to break open structures, to make everything fluid"?

I'm no Armani, but I do think a man's suit needs to come out of what he believes in and look like it is part of his story and his life. It shouldn't sit on him like an inert imposition. A suit needs to take on the life of the man who wears it, but it should give the man something as well.

I like the way Mackenzie puts it when she writes that Armani's lines are a "reaction against hierarchy, a distrust of conformity and rigidity in all its incarnations. As a child he had seen first-hand the perils of a uniform – he must have understood the psychological comfort and equally the danger in such conformity. I asked him if he could sum up the essence of his style. 'To give confidence but not to define the personality,' he said."

Whether dressed in a T-shirt or a suit jacket, who doesn't want to feel that way?

When I ask Bill about removing the padding in a jacket, he says it's not possible to go without it. Modernize customers – especially back in the days when manual labourers and athletes walked through the door – need padding.

"Armanis are good if you have the right figure," he says. "But working people, loggers, farmers, fisherman, they have bigger backs. One arm is larger than the other. They stoop more." Bill stands and demonstrates. "When you're overdeveloped on one side your shoulder drops. Then your waist shifts up on one side to compensate, which means one leg will appear longer than the other. A bad tailor, a lazy tailor, will make one pant leg shorter to compensate, but the proper way is to angle the waistline to visually correct the posture."

As I ponder whether to excise the shoulder pads, I realize that Bill Wong and Giorgio Armani are not as different as I first thought. Though they are worlds away from each other, they share in the same work of making clothes that compensate for the deficiencies in a man's life. Whether a man seeks physical symmetry or a sense of freedom and moral agency, the right suit can provide him with a psychic prosthetic and a rectifying force field.

I'm not sure if I can articulate what I need or find missing in my father's suit. But it feels right to unload the coat, to make it lighter, softer. It needs to try less. So I excise the shoulder pads. Then I begin the task of narrowing the shoulders. I redraw the top of the armhole and use my shears to take off the extra inches. Before, the shoulders winged off and held my sleeves away from my body. Now, the seams will sit right on my shoulder.

I thought I could avoid opening up the lining but I can't. Working from the outside with a ladder stitch isn't going to do the trick; it doesn't allow me to make the straight, hard seams needed to define the shoulders. I attach the sleeves from the inside. There's extra work now to close the lining again but it's all worth it. I feel better knowing the pads aren't there. The jacket now feels light as a feather. I go to look in the bathroom mirror. My head looks enormous.

IN LATE WINTER OF 1983, MY FATHER STARTED accepting ownership shares in restaurants that couldn't pay him for his consultancy work. He became partial owner of businesses worth nothing except for the equipment he purchased on his clients' behalf and now owed money on. If things didn't improve we would soon face bankruptcy, a concept I didn't understand, but I remember listening to my mother who, when she found the pressure too much, would sometimes go into private tirades as she cooked or cleaned the kitchen. She would move from the counter to the table, speaking to no one but nevertheless repeating in detail the purchases my father never should have made and the bills that still needed to be paid. One time, I put it to her simply, "We don't have enough money?"

"What do you think? It doesn't grow on trees."

Then one evening my father came home and informed the family we were now the owners of a cottage in the Laurentians, a range of low mountains north of Montreal dotted with tiny ski villages. I don't know how my father expected us to respond to his announcement, but he was disappointed. The whole family was shocked. I remember watching him standing in the dining room, looking so excited. I felt my throat constrict. I thought I was suffocating. "Dad, we can't afford it."

My father roared, "How would you know anything about what we can and can't afford?" Then he looked at my mother. "She is telling you bullshit."

My mother's own anger surfaced. "I don't care. Do what you want. It's your business."

I saw the frustration on my father's face overtaken by hopelessness. He let out a breath and turned to my mother but she had already slipped back into the kitchen, where it sounded like she was intent on banging pots together rather than putting them away. I went back to my room and lay on my bed and stared at the ceiling, thinking about how I wanted nothing more than a normal family.

That weekend we drove up to the Laurentians to spend our first weekend at the cottage. It was a low-lying white-stuccoed rancher on the north side of a mountain, where even at noon it sat under a deep cold shadow. The driveway was covered with snow, so we had to park on the road far below. We grabbed our bags and groceries and climbed up the path, where the snow came up to my waist. Despite the grim situation, everyone was eager to see the place. I had been to a friend's family cottage once before. They had a sunny A-frame made of broad wood planks, and a roaring fireplace where we ate melted raclette cheese on potatoes with pickled onions and gherkins. It was cosy. Maybe our cottage could be the same.

We worked our way through the deep snow, 125 steps up the hill to the front porch, and with each step everyone became more excited. I was hoping for bright rustic floorboards with colourful woven carpets. Perhaps the walls would smell of cedar. We would spend hours playing backgammon on the couch. When my father unlocked the door to our cottage, we found a long, dark, mildewy cavern. A tired grey carpet covered the floor. The air was so cold I could see my breath. There was no running water. The pipes had frozen. When I asked my father where the thermostat was, he said the furnace had no oil. "But look at this," he said. "Two stone fireplaces." He found wood under the porch but it took a long time to get the logs burning. Wet, they made disapproving hisses in the fireplace. Gradually, the house warmed. My father declared that he and I would work on the pipes tomorrow. But for now, he would get a celebratory bottle of wine for lunch.

The cottage had seven bedrooms but we spent our first night sleeping in front of the fireplace in our sleeping bags. The next morning my father and I went to the local hardware store and bought lengths of copper pipe and soldering equipment. I spent the rest of the day on my back in the dark with a flashlight under my arm, lying on the frozen soil of the basement crawlspace fixing leaks. For the rest of that winter, when my father asked if we wanted to go to the cottage, I would always beg him to let me stay at home.

Spring came early that year. My friends and I spent hours breaking up the ice on one another's driveways with pickaxes, spades, and the heels of our boots. I was clearing the last of the ice on our driveway when a truck pulled up to the house. Three men had come to take our living room furniture away. We owned a couch, two armchairs, a love-seat, and a coffee table made of rosewood. Carved into the wood were goldfish ponds and pagodas, maidens and ancient bald-headed scholars walking along a garden path. Red silk covered the cushions and embroidered dragons snaked across them. The children were rarely allowed to sit in the living room, which was never a pleasant experience in any case. The cushions were slippery; if I leaned back into the chair my cushion would slide out from under me.

My mother refused to let the men into the house. She grabbed the door jamb and braced her arms. She kept saying, "No." Looking back, I'm not sure why there wasn't a bailiff or sheriff present. Perhaps my father had received a telephone call from a debt collector at the office. Perhaps the man had threatened to take away our furniture and my father had called what he thought was the agent's bluff by saying, "Go right ahead. Do it." Only the agent hadn't been bluffing. However, my mother stood firm. The repossession men left with an empty truck. A few days later, sometime between my leaving for school and coming home, the furniture disappeared. All that remained were the impressions left by the furniture on the carpet. My father had made an arrangement with another Chinese family. They would hold onto the pieces until our money situation improved.

After the cottage, my father came home maybe only once or twice a week. He was now living at the office. Nights in the house became calmer. One night, lying in bed, I began to fantasize about what life would be like if we had a normal father. He would come home on time for dinner and sober. He would slip out of his suits and change into a polo shirt and rugby pants, and we'd watch *Three's Company* together in the basement or load the VCR and watch *Caddyshack* for the seventieth time. He would have a job I could explain. He'd be a teacher or even a waiter. I know I would have been happier if he were just a waiter. I would no longer have to wonder why my friends' fathers always came home but mine didn't. I didn't want late-night presents from him anymore. I could do without the midnight meals of smoked meat sandwiches and without the new cars and the surprise cottages that were too large to heat in winter. I wanted his voice to sound clear, not slurred. I wanted him to be happy. I prayed for it, because if he was happy, maybe there wouldn't be anything to fear. I didn't want to be afraid of my father hurting my mother anymore, or imagine what it would mean to confront him. The next morning I went into my parents' room to see if he had come home. Then I looked in the basement, but he wasn't on the couch or under the ping-pong table. Tammy and I said not a word about him to each other. We acted like everything was normal. I ate breakfast and went to school and by the second bell I had forgotten about him.

After five nights without him coming home, a new thought occurred to me. Maybe this was it. Maybe he would never come home. Maybe I could now go to sleep and not have to worry about being woken up by offers of late-night meals or surprise gifts, or the sound of fighting. There would be no more nights of loud music. No more of anything. I would become the man of the house. This was something I had not considered before. Looking back, it seems ridiculous that I thought it would be possible to replace my father. But we could do without him.

That night, I went to bed in utter peace. I was certain my father would never come home again. And somehow, the loss of expectation had burst the bubble of yearning that had become more desperate as my family's situation grew worse. Perhaps he had hit rock bottom, but we would sink no further.

Around eleven, I heard the front door swing open and bang into the wall. Then heavy footsteps came over the threshold. The coat hangers rattled. He must have been shaking snow off his leather loafers. His slow scrape-thud walk changed to heavy padding as he moved from the foyer to the carpeted hallway. The refrigerator door opened then closed. I heard him unwrap some food. A plate rattled on the counter. From all these sounds I was able to measure the depths of his drunkenness and the darkness of his mood. When I heard him carelessly toss the plate onto the counter, I became enraged.

If I had left him alone, if I had simply stayed in bed, I would have heard his feet shuffle and slide downstairs. He was near dead-drunk and he would have soon settled into a heavy stupor. But I got out of bed.

He was halfway down the stairs when I called out to him from the hallway. "Hey, Dad. Where've you been?"

"I've been working." His voice was thick and leaden. He hadn't been working at all.

"Why are you never home?"

"What? I always come home."

But that's not what I meant. I wanted him to tell me why

he never came home sober. Why couldn't he be happy? What did we do to make him so unhappy? Why did he hurt Mum? Most importantly, I wanted him to tell me I would not become like him.

Instead I said, "I miss you."

And with those words, I did. I wanted him to stop and turn at the bottom of the stairs and, although I was nearly a man, I wanted him to hold my hand and walk me back to bed. I wanted him to promise to never strike my mother or raise his voice again. I wanted him to say, "I'm sorry. I miss you too."

He went into a rage.

"You have no idea how hard I'm working."

"Who do you think is putting food on the table?"

"Who do you think is paying for the cottage?"

"Where do you think our cars come from?"

"You little shit. You're a fucking ingrate. What do you want from me? I grew up with nothing. I didn't have a father. I didn't have a mother. You don't have to work. What do you want now?"

"I don't want anything. I want you."

He came up the stairs and pushed me into the kitchen. He raised his arms to strike me, something he had never done before. Suddenly my mother jumped in between us. Our argument had woken her.

"Don't touch him!"

"You love them so much. Watch what I do to them!"

She told me to run. I opened the kitchen door that led to the side of the house and stepped outside. My father moved towards me but my mother blocked his way. Then she raised her arms to protect herself. Turned her body away from an impending blow. Time slowed. Then froze.

My parents are in the kitchen. The kitchen is yellow. My father holds a Moulinex mixer blade in his hand. He delicately twirls the two curved blades between his fingers as if it were a toy. It reminds me of a spinning top. His face becomes focused with intent. There is no longer any anger, just calculation. He means to throw it.

I let go of the screen door and I run. I'm barefoot and in pyjamas. I don't feel the stones beneath my feet. I feel a thrill. I have never run so fast before and all I am thinking is how fast I am, running one hundred metres barefoot in thirteen seconds. I am running fast, running faster now. I am thirteen. I am a coward. And I wish I had never been born.

The first task of the salesman lies in careful observation, in the process which is sometimes known as "sizing up." He must become a veritable Sherlock Holmes in his endeavour to notice every detail in the customer's appearance and manner which will enable him to deduce his tastes, habits, and financial standing. Much can be learned from the first glance; his age, his size, his probable occupation, his general tidiness or otherwise. This information must be supplemented by tactful questions and conversation; and every effort should be made to get the customer to talk about himself.

H.J. Chappell, "Salesmanship for Tailors"

THE TERM IS HYPERVIGILANCE. IT IS A SKILL DEVELOPED by children who either witness abuse or are victims themselves. They are able to detect small changes in facial expressions and mood in anticipation of conflict and danger. They often have a strong desire to please others to ward off confrontation, but once it starts they immediately switch to the offensive. They don't back down. I should know. I'm blessed and cursed with this trait.

Reporters are often known for being insensitive, a quality that can make them good at their job. It doesn't mean they are boors; it means they don't take rejection to heart. If their questions make people feel uncomfortable, good reporters will think "tough noogies."

I was good because I was oversensitive. I could feel when someone was clamming up or willing to share. I was able to ask questions and draw out answers when other reporters could not. For example, I once asked a highly decorated officer who had fought twenty battles in Afghanistan (he liked to call them "kinetic operations") what it was like to kill someone. I didn't ask what it was like to be in combat or to see action so many times. No, I asked him what it was like to kill another man. The answer, in short, was "not very nice." I could feel he wanted to get beyond the REMF (rear-echelon motherfucker) bullshit jargon he learned in officer school and was coached to spew by public relations specialists. Ten minutes into our conversation, I knew he needed to tell me something real about his experience.

Hypervigilance also cuts the other way. It makes me nervous or afraid. Any change of mood, any passing cloud of pique either sends me into a defensive, ready-to-fight posture or makes me want to run away. I have the sudden urge to placate or beat the person into the ground. Working in an office, where I'm forced to be around many people, can sometimes be unbearable. There are too many moods and needs to negotiate. My senses become overloaded. The only time I can relax and be focused on the task at hand is when I've worked with a team for a long time and I trust them. Otherwise, I feel isolated and alone, always on the outside of what seems to be a secret ongoing conversation.

Hypervigilance makes me highly attuned to people who

feel the same way. I'm attracted to loners and quiet types. If they fall into an awkward silence, I'll fill the air with my own prattle. If they are unhappy or anxious, I can't help myself, I am compelled to go out of my way to help them even if it's none of my business.

What does this have to do with tailoring? Well, it turns out my sensitivities make me one hell of a salesman. As the new front-of-store man at Modernize, I'm responsible for dealing with new clientele, those young men in black-rimmed eyeglasses, skinny jeans, and sneakers who have recently become interested in suits.

"What do you call them, JJ?"

"Sometimes they're called hipsters, Bill."

"Ah, I see. Well, when a young man comes in when I'm busy, you can make yourself useful, see. You can talk to them. Let them know what we can do for them."

Walking into a tailor's shop can be intimidating. For many young men, it will be the first time they've ever stepped into one. Often, the tailors will be very old, like Bill and Jack, old enough to be their grandfathers. Plus the young men come with visions in their heads, mental images snipped from GQ and Esquire, music videos and movies – cultural references far beyond an older tailor's knowledge. Sure, if you say you're looking for a little Sean Connery or Dean Martin in your made-to-measure, he can help you. Even if you drop Steve McQueen, you'll still be talking the same language. But if you tell an older tailor you want to wear your suit with a pair of Cons, he might ask you what line of work forces you to spend your days with prison inmates. If you say Kanye (as in West), he might think of Nairobi. If you say preppy with a touch of hip hop, he may make you a suit that says bebop. There will be a generation gap. This is where I come in at Modernize. I play the role of envoy.

Because many of the men who come into the shop are so young, my job is to make them feel comfortable in our very old shop. The first thing I try to do is identify whether they want a single- or double-breasted jacket. Then it's on to the number of buttons (one, two, or three – I won't sell you four), the type of lapel (notched or peaked) and venting (no vent, single vent, or side vents).

Then comes the hard part: picking fabric. The shop has hundreds of bolts and unless the customer is after the most basic of blue suits, he can spend hours picking the right fabric. To speed things up, I maintain a collection of vintage bolts, one-of-a-kind fabrics from defunct English mills, which I like to call "the stash." If I show a young man the stash, he will see more vivid and deeper blues than he's ever seen before. The touch of these bolts is softer than soft. By the time I tell him he won't find an inch of this fabric anywhere else – and I mean it, it isn't BS – he doesn't stand a chance. He'll be hooked. So I'm careful not to overwhelm a man with the sartorial firepower at my disposal. I really want a customer to walk away with the suit he deserves. I try to dance with him, find out where he's coming from, anticipate his anxieties, and find a way to make him absolutely sure about his commitment. Like I said, I'm hypervigilant.

So far, in my first month of helping Bill out as a front-of-store man, I've sold seven suits. Most of the customers want side vents and working buttons on the sleeves. Working buttons used to be a sign of hand-tailoring, so I encourage customers to choose this option but Park hates it. We make more money with working buttons, but now he is up to his neck with coatmaking orders. He is not happy with me because I still haven't learned to sew properly, I have yet to even help attach buttons, and now I've increased his workload but can't help him deliver. He's losing patience with me, which I understand. Nobody is young in the shop except for me and I don't have the skills to relieve the pressure. I've been ordered not to take in any more orders until July.

Even so, I'm beginning to think I can make a go of tailoring. To really earn my keep here, I'd have to sell around sixteen suits a month. Productivity would have to go up — Park would then be the bottleneck. I'm thinking I should tell Bill to raise the price of a suit to $1,000. We could make fewer suits and I could finally earn a wage. If I sound cocky, it's because I am. I'm not proud of it. I've never been very good with keeping my place in the order of things. And a meticulous and responsible man like Park knows I represent chaos, disruption, and possibly disaster.

For example, the other day, Rodney came in with a special project. Rodney, an English fashion marketer living in Vancouver, wanted a copy of a pair of pants by high-concept fashion designer Alexandre Plokhov of Cloak in New York. The only guide Rodney brought in for us was a tiny picture from a Japanese fashion magazine. The pants were grey with wide legs. On one side there seemed to be an enormous bulge. We spent weeks trying to determine the cause of the bulge. I told Bill it appears to be from massive box pleats that billow at the knees. Bill disagreed. He believed it was a giant cargo pocket and proceeded to make the pants himself. Then Rodney came in for the moment of truth. Both Bill and I waited by the trifold mirror as he came out of the changing room. The pants looked ridiculous. The bulge was a cancerous growth. Rodney could stuff a skateboard into the pocket.

Bill manoeuvred Rodney in front of the mirror so he could pin up the hem.

"Looks good, looks good," said Bill.

Rodney said, "I really like it."

Then I piped in. "The pocket. Do you like the scale?"

Rodney loved it.

"Would you like us to make it smaller?"

"Why would I want that?" It was exactly what he was looking for.

Bill stepped between me and Rodney. "I'll fix the hem and you can pick it up tomorrow."

When Rodney left, Bill leaned against the cutting table. He waited for the echo of the shop bell to fade.

"That was really stupid."

What did I do wrong?

"He liked the pants. That's what he wanted. You tried to make him change the pants."

"The pockets were so huge."

"It doesn't matter. You're not a fashion designer. This isn't a design studio. You're not here to tell people how to dress."

Bill's vehemence floored me. I began to think about how I had become too comfortable in the shop. A sense of dread came over me, the kind that I only ever felt with my father when I had done something wrong. Here I was, a grown man feeling like a little kid again. I could hear my father's voice in my head, chastising me. *Why don't you pay attention? Why don't you focus? This is serious.* It was the word *stupid.* My father used to call me that. And that's how I felt. I was sure Bill was going to fire me.

Instead Bill said, "You should focus on practising to make pockets."

After Bill left to go on an errand, Jack, who had watched the whole scene, shuffled over to me, picking at a loose thread on a pant hem, trying to look nonchalant. He knew I was crushed.

"Tailoring is a hard business. You don't want to do a job twice. If I had to fix every little mistake, I wouldn't get any work done."

"I'm sorry, I just wasn't thinking."

"No big deal," Jack said in his wistful singsong voice and then he shuffled back to his sewing machine.

I took this as a signal to settle behind mine. As I set the foot down, telling myself to focus on making the straightest and steadiest line of stitches ever, the number one rule of salesmanship repeated in my head: "The customer is always right." And so is your master tailor.

I RAN TO JIMMY AND SHANNON BENNETT'S HOUSE.
Though two years younger, Jimmy was my playmate.
Tammy and Shannon were best friends. Their mother, whom
I still call Mrs. B., also got along well with my mother.

It was Mrs. B. who told me, decades later, what happened
that night. When I came in she sat me down in their kitchen
and made me tea and a peanut butter sandwich. Mr. B. put
me to bed in Jimmy's room. Jimmy was having a sleepover
at a classmate's. I was already in pyjamas. I remember pacing
the room, looking at his blue *Star Wars* linens and curtains,
and the Han Solo figurine on his wooden bookcase. I have
no distinct memory of ever setting foot into my own
bedroom again.

In the morning, Mr. B. sat at the edge of the bed.

"Your father is asleep in the house."

"What about Aimee and Lenny?"

"They're in the house with him but they're okay."

He told me Tammy had spent the night sleeping in

Shannon's room. My mother was in the hospital but she was okay, too.

"We had a talk with your mom, and Tammy is going to live with us. Aimee and Lenny are going to stay with your dad."

I didn't understand. Mr. B. explained my father was going to take them to live in the cottage in the Laurentians. I had a choice to make. I could move with my younger brother and sister – and my father. Or I could live with the Bennetts.

To me the Bennetts were the perfect family. At Christmas time, their tree – not an artificial one but a real spruce tree – was surrounded by a mountainous gathering of boxes. Mrs. B. made shortbread cookies and fruitcake drenched in rum. Mr. B. came home for dinner every night and I would often join them. My favourite meal was beef stew with Yorkshire pudding. Mrs. B. would ladle out the stew from a gleaming stainless stockpot. At our home, supper was dished out from a blackened and beaten wok. I wanted to stay. Although I don't remember saying it, Mrs. B. told me that what I said to Mr. B. was, "But who is going to watch Aimee and Lenny?" At the time Aimee was only ten, and Lenny was in kindergarten. "I have to take care of them."

⚖

The move happened fast. Within days, we had packed our essential belongings. I moved with my clothes stuffed into a green garbage bag. I kept no toys except for Willy the Worm, a purple toy snake with a missing plastic eye. I was forced to leave my box of comic books behind with Paquito, who promised to take care of them. I had classic back issues of *Captain America*, and a set of *Superboy and the Legion of Super-Heroes* comics. My father had given them to me when I had just started to learn how to read. They had come in a flat blue box wrapped in tissue paper. It is one of my fondest memories I have of my father, even though it was probably my mother who went to the used bookstore to buy them. The only other things I managed to hold onto were a few music cassettes, including my copy of U2's *War*, and a Sanyo C5 portable radio cassette stereo. Whatever my father could not shove into the car was either thrown away or left behind. It would be years before I understood that our home had been sold to pay my father's debts.

The only news of my mother we received (it may have been from an aunt) was that she had been released from hospital and was now living at the Salvation Army hostel in downtown Montreal. She had not pressed charges. There was no indication from my father or from any other adult as to whether my mother would reunite with us. We children didn't wonder or speculate. Again we did not talk about her. We were too frightened. It was as if she were dead. She had simply disappeared.

Tammy refused to come back into the house. Before we left, I took her clothes and her guitar over to the Bennetts', where she was now bunking with Shannon. The Bennetts drew back, leaving the two of us alone in the front hall. Tammy said, "Take care, okay."

I suppose I should have felt sad that she wasn't coming with us, but I didn't. She was the lucky one. She would get to stay in our hometown and finish the year at our high school. I was the one taking the long walk to my father's car, the engine running.

I can still hear the crinkle of the cold garbage bags filled with clothes on my lap as we drove away from our house. Sheena lay at my feet in the front seat. As my father drove up the highway to the Laurentians, everything that had been part of our life fell behind and receded to the horizon.

It was evening by the time we arrived at the cottage. The driveway was still snowbound. From the road, we climbed the endless stairs to reach the front door.

With the exception of the master bedroom, I had the choice of one of the six bedrooms at the cottage. All of them cold. I picked the room farthest from where my father slept.

⌂

My father registered Aimee and Lenny at the local elementary school. They would walk to school on their own and come home to an empty house. I spent the remaining months of grade eight at Laurentian Regional High School. I had to catch a school bus at seven in the morning and endure a two-hour tour of every village between Sainte-Adèle and my school, which was thirty miles away. I would return to the cottage at five o'clock to find Aimee and Lenny watching television. For supper, I would heat up cans of beans or beef stew. Sometimes I cooked hot dogs or made bowls of instant ramen noodles. After dinner I would light a fire. Then I would grab a big blanket and we would push the couch that had come with the cottage close to the fireplace so we could prop our feet up on the flagstone hearth. I would make Aimee and Lenny snuggle with me on the couch under the blanket, and we would listen to U2 until they fell asleep. We never saw our father come home and he would still be asleep in the mornings when we left for school.

My father still drank but he no longer had my mother to focus his anger and frustrations on. Instead, he targeted Sheena, our black Labrador. He had always been cruel to her. On walks, if she became tangled on a signpost or a sapling, my father would pull on the leash to force her to come around instead of simply letting go. She was a gentle dog who never snapped at any of the children. I loved it when she slept in bed with me. Back in the old house, Aimee and I used to argue over who would have her for the night. Sheena was so obedient my mother could point to the field across the street, and she would run to the field, do her business, and then run back to our house without any distraction or detour. All she wanted was to be with us. Sheena, a dog who would come when you called her name and trot by your heel when commanded, never deserved the punishment she received from my father.

One day he no longer allowed Sheena to live in the cottage, banishing her to under the front porch with the fire logs and spring snow. He gave no reason. He simply grabbed her by the collar and brought her under the porch. It had a green door. He opened it, put her in, and locked it. At bedtime, I could still hear her whimpers. When I was sure my father had fallen asleep, I put on a sweater and slippers and sat by the front door. I talked to her until I found it too cold. The next day my father poured her a bowl of food and tied her to a lead.

There's one thing I need you to understand: I have not thought about any of these memories in nearly three decades. There are gaps and vague images and feelings bunched together into a distant corner of my mind. I've worked very hard to put them there, and yet now it seems so important to understand what went on. If I can't unlock the puzzle of my father, what hope is there for me? I see myself becoming more and more like him with every day that passes, but I don't want to be the kind of man he was. I don't drink anymore. I've never smoked. I've never even learned how to drive. These are all things I associate with my father. But then there's our shared interest in clothes.

For years, I denied my father had any influence on me and I fully believed I had created myself. Then he died. Since then the memories have beckoned, though I refused them. But I can't live anymore with the fabric of my childhood riddled with gaps and holes, guilt and shame. I don't need to reconcile all the contradictions. I'm not sure how one even mends such things, and I'm certainly not looking for anything as pitiful as closure. But I will admit that in those missing pieces are memories of my father, and that he is a part of me.

I telephone Aimee to see what she recalls. "I try not to remember anything about back then," she says.

She tells me she doesn't have any distinct memories of that time. But when I press, she tells me about how she and Lenny would disobey our father and let Sheena into the house after school. They would keep lookout just in case he came home early. One day they were caught. My father did not say a word to them. Instead he led Sheena into the car and drove away. He came back an hour later without her. Again, we kept quiet. None of us dared ask where they had gone. We could only guess Sheena's fate.

Maybe one reason why we have such poor recollections is it seemed there was nothing permanent in our lives. Our dog, our home, our sister, our mother all disappeared in an instant. If things so important could vanish like that, how could anything endure or be memorable?

I lived in an increasingly narrow world in the spring of 1983. My senses recorded only those things that were a few feet away from me. There was Aimee, Lenny, the creak of my bed, the cold floor, the slow melt of the snow in the backyard, my U2 tape, and hardly anything else. There was no distance or future. Nothing else existed. I made no friends. I had no sense of time passing. I had no longing. If I try to summon sounds or voices from that period, I can't hear my father at all. I hear mostly the hissing of wet logs in the fireplace, the rustle of the duvet, and the lurching squeak of the cassette player. And one night, as the embers died and the last song faded on the tape, Aimee blurting out, "I'm glad they're not together."

In spite of what artists and lovers of the unique and the strange in the Japanese may say, the natives themselves understand human nature and hold true the philosophy of clothes. Their great ambition is to be treated as men, as gentlemen, and as the equals of Occidentals. In their antiquated garb they knew that they or their country would never be taken seriously.

William Elliot Griffis, *The Mikado* (1915)

TODAY, IN VANCOUVER, I CAME ACROSS TWO REAL-life Japanese salarymen. Salarymen or *sararīman* are Japanese white-collar workers who are hired for life by corporations or government bureaucracies. Like tailors, they are a dying breed. The number of salarymen has decreased over the last decade, as they have been replaced by temporary workers whom employers feel no qualms about firing or laying off.

Despite representing Japan's best and brightest, salarymen are often portrayed in film and fiction as alienated, enslaved drones who love karaoke and after-hours drinking binges. Salarymen embody self-sacrifice, compliance to hierarchy, and the elevation of one's corporation and country above all else. Their dedication is legendary. In some cases, it has proven to be lethal. In 1994, the Japanese Ministry of Health, Labour and Welfare was forced to establish special hotlines to deal with *karōshi* – literally "sudden death from overworking." Between 2002 and 2004, roughly fifteen hundred cases of mental distress, strokes, heart attacks, and suicides were officially attributed to *karōshi* syndrome. The life of a salaryman is not an easy one.

With the collapse of the Japanese economy in 1991 and the ensuing two decades of lacklustre performance known as the Lost Years, the term *salaryman* has become a pejorative. The younger generation of Japanese workers, those twenty-something Japanese who came of age during the Lost Years, now see the treasured titles, advancements, and raises that signalled salaryman success as secondary to quality of life.

The way salarymen wear their suits has also shifted over the years. For example, in the 1960s, "securities salesmen were ordered to wear a wool jacket in the steamiest summer weather when visiting clients, so that sweat stains formed large blotches on the back and under the arms. This was how they made their appeal of sincerity and dedication." In the 1990s, after the economic bubble burst, one Japanese report noted that salaryman style favoured "battered shoes over new; dark colors over bright; polyester over natural cotton." Recession suit wearers could not "look too good or be too comfortable. . . . Men must look dark and seamy if only in deference to the times and the clients." Suits, back then, had to reflect the collective experience. Individual expression, let alone individual comfort, was beside the point. Now, while the economy has yet to recover, the suit in Japan has moved beyond being a form of sartorial self-flagellation.

My Japanese salarymen were on the train. They were young and wearing blue suits. (All salarymen, it would seem, wear dark suits.) What I noticed about this pair was how incredibly correct their suits appeared. The jacket sleeves fell short enough to reveal a quarter-inch of shirt cuff. The ties were perfectly knotted with a dimple. Their two-button jackets neatly buttoned (remember, just the top button) gave a nice waist suppression, emphasizing a slender yet strong upper body and a trim mid-section. They were perfectly dressed but not dull. The guy on the left wore a pair of precise, chisel-toed shoes by, I would guess, Prada and a braided leather bracelet on his wrist. The salaryman on the right had long, layered, curling hair that brushed the shoulders and the border of corporate respectability. He was also cultivating a five-day beard in the manner of the Seattle Mariners All-Star right fielder, Ichiro Suzuki. Nothing dull at all. The jaunty details elevated their suits into masterpieces of individuality in ways I seldom see among young North American men. There was nothing studied or forced or derivative about their appearance. To me it seemed so contemporary and uncanny.

The anthropologist Dorinne Kondo once cited an observation made by Japanese novelist Yugen Matsumura that sticks with me:

From that moment [in 1867] the importation of a "Western sensibility" began. The men who had been at fashion's cutting edge successfully adapted their bodies to the demands of Western clothing. In this era these men achieved the same success with their economic endeavours. Now, if

you look at their photographs – men who had only a short history of acquaintance with Western dress – you immediately notice their surprisingly fresh, stylish way of wearing the clothes. It's a strange shock to see that these Japanese men whose inner spirit was far from tranquil, whose spirit led them to do things like commit *seppuku*, were far more stylish than the men of today, who wear Western fashions in a Western way.

The moment Muramatsu refers to is the Meiji Restoration, named after Emperor Meiji, who ascended to the throne in 1867 at the age of fourteen and ruled until 1912. Under

Emperor Meiji, Japan entered a long period of intense Westernization in defiance of the legacy of his father, Emperor Kōmei, who resisted allowing Western powers to have greater access to Japan. The young Emperor Meiji very quickly made *yofuku*, or European-styled dress, mandatory for the royal court on official business. Eventually the entire civil service was expected to wear frock coats as any Englishman would.

It was during this period of upheaval that Western and Japanese menswear began to come together in startling ways. One surviving photographic image from the years leading to the Meiji period shows a collection of *Kiheitai*

STETSON-LIKE HATS AND MILITARY LONG COATS WTH BRASS BUTTONS
COLLIDE WITH TRADITIONAL TOP KNOTS AND SHAVED PATES.

from Chōshū. These were an unprecedented militia composed of lower-ranked samurai mixed with peasants. Though their goal was to repulse foreign powers and everything they represented from Japan, the fighters were trained in both Japanese fighting arts and Western military drill.

The picture is extraordinary. It is of several rebels, all young men, teens even. And though many resistors to Western encroachment banned *yofuku* in their households and among their servants, in this group portrait the posers don a mélange of *wafuku* or Japanese clothes and *yofuku*. Stetson-like hats and military long coats with brass buttons collide with traditional top knots and shaved pates. One member looks every bit the cowboy. He wears a vest and kerchief and holds a pocket watch out to the camera. On his belt hangs an ornate samurai sword, the *katana*. Somehow the salarymen on the train and the young samurai I find in this 140-year-old photograph are connected in their insistence on being themselves – even in the face of cultural and historical pressures.

&

I have gone about altering my father's suit the wrong way.

I have been altering it piece by piece, element by element, without understanding the whole of the suit or even the why. I have tried to change the suit based on what I don't want the suit to be instead of understanding what I need it to be.

What do I need it to be? What is the identity I seek and wish to form with this suit? Andre Dubus III once said that trying not to be your father makes you more like your father. But you can't blame me for trying.

As my only term at Laurentian Regional High School came to an end, my father made an announcement. We were moving again. He had sold the cottage to settle the last of his debts. But this time he had a plan. He had leased a restaurant in a town called Rigaud. And Tammy, who had just finished her academic year and had had a change of heart, would be moving there with us.

The restaurant was in a hotel off the highway between Montreal and Toronto. It was surrounded by a parking lot of gravel and broken asphalt. The dominant features of the interior were brown carpet and a wooden screen of spindles that divided the dining area into two sections. My father planned to serve classic Canadian-Chinese fare like egg rolls, fried rice, and bland wonton soup to the locals. Next door was a bar, its patrons consisting of bikers, strippers, part-time prostitutes, rummies, and drifters.

There was no big fanfare when Tammy returned to the family, the great silence and active forgetting were maintained as if we were a submarine crew running silent and deep. It went unsaid, but I was happy to see her again. She would live with Aimee, Lenny, and me in one of the hotel suites. There were three beds: the girls slept on twin beds in the back part of the suite, Len slept on another twin bed in the front room, while I slept on the same lawn lounger I had once used to watch shooting stars. Our father had a room down the hall.

Aimee told me recently the hotel scared her at first. Even I knew it was no place to bring up young children, but Aimee has a clearer image of the hotel. At night, she often heard fights in the hallways among the semi-permanent residents and guests. There were mornings when she would wake up to find the hallway walls dented by fists and smeared with blood. I never noticed. While Tammy, Aimee, and Lenny spent their days watching television, I had to keep odd hours. As the eldest son, it was my duty to wake up at eleven and go down-stairs to the restaurant. My father could handle the early tables on his own but he needed me for the lunchtime rush.

My father would be in the kitchen prepping food. Often I found him standing over a cauldron of weak broth, pouring cups of white MSG crystals into it. We barely spoke to each other. What could I say to him? I had found another reason to be angry with him. He was a good cook, but the way he prepared food at the restaurant was despicable. He would make me preboil pasta and then douse it in cold water when it was slow (most of our customers arrived in the late morning to eat egg rolls as a salve for hangovers, or late at night). Then I would load the noodles into large gallon drums and store them in the walk-in refrigerator. Even then I knew this was wrong. The pasta should have been cooked, if not fresh to order, at least prior to each meal service. He cut other corners. For crispy chow mein noodles, he poured flavoured noodles straight from the cellophane bag into the wok instead of deep-frying fresh noodles. The customers didn't notice the difference, but my father knew better, which made me sad. In fact, he had taught me better, and watching him cheat the world of what he knew to be right made me want to scream, but I kept silent. Perhaps he avoided talking to me for the same reason.

My job as the cook's assistant, busboy, and dishwasher kept me up late into the night, and I usually hit the sack at two or three a.m. I recall one time when the restaurant had been particularly busy – a touring troupe of strippers had set up shop at the bar for the weekend and they drew quite a crowd. That night I had to work through a mountain of dishes, and I remember watching the clock over the freezer. The bar was supposed to shut at two but the music still thumped next door. I hoped they would clear out in a half-hour, which meant it would be an hour before I could collect all the dishes, scrape and load them, and then another hour of sweeping and mopping the floor. For some reason, my father, who had already gone upstairs after the last order, left me with dozens of pots and pans to scrub on my own. That was another hour. When I was done, instead of going upstairs to sleep, I went outside. The sun was orange-red and rising. It was my fourteenth birthday. "Today," I thought to myself, despite my thin frame and the helpless feeling of smallness inside me, "I am a man."

I walked along the main road and sat on a rail bridge spanning a polluted creek. All this was because of my father.

It was his road and this was where it had taken us. There were no suits. No valets. There were no secret back doors to the finest kitchens in the city. What was the point of working all those extra hours to afford Bally loafers when we were now living in Rigaud, a town no one ever stopped in and that had only one Chinese restaurant – ours.

That was the moment when I made the promise all sons make to themselves: I would never be like my father. My children would be around me all the time and I would never let them down. But even as I made that vow I felt its hollow ring.

That summer, I detected in my father remorse for what he had done to us. The collapse of our family had aged him. He had started to lose his hair. The energy and the violence he once held in his body had seeped away. He used to have the body of a middleweight boxer or a football scatback, but now he seemed to sag. A belly began to hang off his frame. My father's wardrobe also eroded. He no longer wore suits or nice shoes. You don't need calfskin loafers when you're working a wok and deep fryer. My father's suits were replaced by pleated-front khakis, white sneakers splattered with grease and caked with food crumbs, and thrift-store short-sleeved shirts embroidered with corporate logos that had nothing to do with his life.

In retrospect, I can see my father tried to do right. He stopped drinking. He no longer disappeared for days at a time. He kept his temper in check. In fact, it may have evaporated completely. I have no clue as to whether or not we made any money running the restaurant, but we never went hungry. We probably ate too much rice gruel or congee than was nutritionally sound, but I think my father made it as a way of cultivating his bunker mentality. We kids didn't really know what to make of the situation. We just settled in and did the only thing we could. We clung to one another.

It's not so complicated to dress well. You just need to find the right information for you. That's the difficult part of it.

Alan Flusser, in discussion with the author

I'LL ADMIT I'M NOT THE BEST SALESMAN IN THE world, but I love the action of working the front end. I like how I can change a customer's initial anxiety and desperation into excitement. Younger customers especially deserve to feel excited. Think about it. When a young man summons the courage to walk into a strange little shop like ours because he wants to own something different, something special, he deserves to get it.

As I've said, most men of my generation have never been inside a tailor's shop. I'm not talking about an alterationist's storefront, where someone pays the bills by hemming jeans and fixing sleeve lengths. I mean a place of business dedicated to measuring men, cutting bolts of wool, and making suits. Two generations ago, the man most likely to steer you into a tailor's shop was your father. With that sartorial chain mostly broken, the know-how has fallen into obscurity.

Nevertheless, I see men younger than me coming in. They wind themselves up and hold their breath and plunge in. What drives them is a deep desperate need. It is always the same.

You might think this would make the novice suit buyer an impossible customer, because he is after the ineffable. And trust me, he is. I can see the perplexed look on his face. He holds in his head a tight knot of ideas about manhood, fatherhood, success, failure, class, beauty, conformity, anonymity, and individuality. If he brings in his father's suit, I show him how it tells the tale of the man who wore it and how it will also tell the story of the man who will wear it in the future. He always perks up when I say that.

I obviously know how he feels.

I understand how so many voices can speak through a suit, how a suit can seem at once clumsy and too formal. I know suits are quick to read yet hard to understand. It doesn't matter if you wear a suit every day, it's still an arcane, mysterious item.

But I know what you want. Not to burst the bubble of your individuality, but if you walk into our shop and you were born after 1980, I'm going to bet with good odds in my favour you are walking in with an image in your mind that springs from one man. You might not know his name, but the clothes he has designed since the late 1990s have changed the look of men's suits and he is the number one reason suits are regaining popularity. His name is Hedi Slimane.

In 1997, Hedi Slimane became the head designer for Yves Saint Laurent's ready-to-wear line for men called Rive Gauche. At the time, suits were of the Armani cut, big, blousy, and, it occurred to Slimane, overblown. As one GQ writer put it, the suit had become a cliché: "It seems everyone had discovered crepey Milanese tailoring and assumed that the projection of masculinity was a simple business of donning a big suit like so much gladiator gear – then slicking the hair, smoking cigars and generally blowing hard."

Slimane's response in his collections for Rive Gauche and, later, Homme Dior was to narrow the shoulders, raise the armholes, and narrow the sleeves. He wanted trousers "to cut like a knife." He did all that he could to slim down the suit and attracted a following among Hollywood actors and musicians. Even the formerly stocky Karl Lagerfeld, the designer of Chanel, admitted he lost weight so he could fit in one of Slimane's suits: "Yes, it's true. They look best in size 44 and 46 [European equivalents of 34 and 36 chest sizes], so I had to go down to get the smallest size because everything looks best in fashion in the smaller sizes."

Slimane has confessed his famous cut is a result of being unable to find clothes that fit him. He is slender like many of the models he's used over the years, which might not sound terribly innovative for people used to women's fashion but before Slimane male models were often hulking figures. Slimane saw the thin bodies of indie rock musicians as an inspiration. For him, "Fashion = music + youth + sex. This is what my menswear and my style were always about."

His silhouette has been pegged as a harbinger of a revived androgyny and of alternate masculine identities, but it's the close fit, nearly anti-Vitruvian and anti-proportional, that continues to attract admirers. And now, everyone from national news anchors to sixteen-year-olds have finally caught up with him.

Even in the most humble department store, one can find a suit cut according to Slimane's vision. It won't be perfect, but the broad strokes will be there. However, the unfortunate part is very few people know what they're doing. Not the shopper and, sadly, not most salespeople or associates.

How do I know this? Well, because today I've gone undercover as a man shopping for a suit. I am lurking around the men's suit section of a department store, observing male shoppers, young and old, and the verdict is in: they are hapless and incompetent. Most men have never learned how to wear a suit, let alone how to buy one. Their fathers never taught them. As Alan Flusser has observed, sometime in the 1960s or 1970s, fathers started dressing like their sons. As a result, two or three generations of men have lost the savoir-faire. Brando, hippy culture, and Casual Fridays have all played their part in the erosion of sartorial knowledge. For all the hullabaloo about the revival of suits, when it comes to the in-the-trenches know-how, most men remain clueless. They don't know what is a proper fit, what can be altered, and what should never be altered in a new suit (shoulders should simply fit; if they don't, move on), or what kind of lapel works best for what kind of body. They know nothing, and this goes for the salespeople too.

In the suit separates section, I notice a high mom-to-son and girlfriend-to-boyfriend ratio. Every man walks in with a woman in tow. Nothing says "I have to do something serious-but-shitty" more clearly than a man dragging his significant other along. If it's a trip to Vegas, guys want to go without the lady, but if it's a trip to buy a suit for a wedding or funeral, suddenly it's together time.

It's the women who are doing the shopping. They are the ones in charge. I see one woman holding up various combinations of shirts and ties to a man's face while he is standing in a suit two sizes too big. The suit is brown. The coat is striped and so are the ties and shirts. Abomination!

Obviously, she must have read in some dog-eared back issue of *O* or *Cosmopolitan* that the best way to upgrade her man's wardrobe is to get him to buy into some stripe-on-stripe-on-stripe action. Is it hot? No, it's not. It's a bloody mess. Mixing and matching shirt and tie patterns is absolutely fine but don't do it when you're trying to buy a suit. It is a distraction and a mistake. I call it the Paint Chip Syndrome. Ladies, you are dealing with a man in a suit. He is not a rec room requiring a fresh coat of paint, new curtains, and upholstery. Put the shirt and tie down and back away from the colour wheel chart for autumn-coloured skin tones.

When shopping for an off-the-rack suit, don't let the tail wag the dog. Never build an "outfit" around a shirt or a tie. Shirts and ties are like tissues. A bit of soup or a freakish paper-shredding accident and they're gone. The suit, if it's dark, will remain and it has to be versatile and hold up under an infinite number of tie-shirt pairings. Shopping for a good suit means understanding proportion, fit, fabric, and finish.

I can barely contain myself. Actually, I don't.

I see a Chinese kid with his mother standing in front of the trifold mirror, craning his neck, trying to come to grips with his prospective suit. It's for his high school graduation. He's excited to see himself in the suit. The suit marks him and makes concrete the fact he is crossing some threshold in his life. I can almost see it. I can also see the gaping vent exposing his bottom and the strange folds of fabric gathering around the collar, a sign he has a very straight and correct back while the suit was designed for someone with a bit of a feral stoop (for the man who drives the ball to the hoop). A cloud of doubt comes over his face. It is a quick cast but I catch it. He knows something is wrong, but he doesn't know what. I feel bad for him and wish there was someone who could help him. But there's only me. I know what he's going through. I know if nobody helps him now he'll be left to cobble together a system of dress from books, Google, and the collation of bad advice from friends and family. And it will never be enough. I know because that's what I had to do. Sometimes I think if I just had ten more minutes with my father — okay, I wouldn't talk to him only about clothes. There'd be a lot for us to talk about, he and I. But maybe he could have passed on a few more sartorial nuggets and mementos, something for me to hang onto, and given me a foundation on which I could build my own sense of style instead of having to build from nothing, because that's what I feel I've done.

Where is this kid's father anyway? I have no choice. Sometimes a reporter has to put down the notepad and take off the figurative fedora. Besides, I can't help myself.

"Do you mind if I help you?"

The mother looks me up and down. I'm wearing a bow tie, which sets off her suspicion. "Do you work here?"

I lie. I tell her yes.

I turn to the boy. "What's your name?"

"Peter," he mumbles.

Peter stands an inch taller. His hair sprouts thick in a shot of black. He has a swimmer's body but for some reason, when I address him, he cowers. I turn to his companion. "And what's Mum's name?"

"My name is Grace. But I'm not his mother. I'm just helping him find a suit." It's my turn to look her up and down. She wears a grey shirt and black leggings. She must be in her mid-forties, only a few years older than me. Then I notice a button pin on her cardigan: "The Prince Charming Project."

It's a charity that helps male teens buy clothes for high school graduation. Many of the boys either come from poor families or have had brushes with police, but they're also survivors. Some have suffered abuse, most live under ministry care. I read once about how they helped one boy complete high school and qualify for a university scholarship all the while living out of his parents' car. The project is intended to reward the boys for getting themselves out of the worst of the worst. The organization buys them a suit, a tie, a pair of shoes, and a couple of shirts so they can go to the graduation dance in high style. It's a beautiful thing.

"Well, I'm JJ," I tell her. "And both of you are in good hands."

I study Peter. He's definitely a size 38 but with big shoulders. "Do you want a suit just for grad night or do you want to wear it for job interviews later?"

"Job interviews." He looks over at Grace, and she nods in agreement.

"It's been really hard looking for a suit," she says. "It's overwhelming. There's so much to choose from."

I pull out a thin two-button suit. It has no vent in the back, which keeps the price down, but also looks quite chic on young men. Peter puts it on. I ask him, "What do you think?"

"I don't know," he says. "What do you think?"

I tell him to lift his arms and move around. The back collar stays nice and flat. There will be no gape when he sits or stands. When his arms hang down, there are no wrinkles on the sleeve. I point all these details out to him.

"Also, you see the back? It's smooth, I mean really smooth. See how it falls smoothly over your rump." *Rump*, the word makes him smile.

"And you look like a perfect 38 to me. It fits perfect. Do you like it?"

"I like it. But how do we make it more fun?"

"Like rock 'n' roll?"

"I guess, yeah." Of course, it's for grad night.

I dash through the shirt and tie section and return with a purple medium-collared shirt, a black bow tie with skulls and crossbones embroidered into the silk, and two pocket squares: one is pink with small white dots and the other has the same skull and bones pattern. Peter goes into the changing room to put on the shirt. When he comes out I throw the bow tie around his neck and begin to knot it. I say, "You okay with the bow tie?"

He cranes his neck to catch a glimpse of himself in the mirror. A small smile begins to crack on his face. "Yeah."

This is when I start to feel a pang of guilt for lying. I know he's never worn a tie before. I can just tell. Yet, here I am, inside this teen's bubble of personal space, and he trusts me. And I've snuck into this moment that is best shared between a father and son.

"Have you ever tied a tie like this before?"

"Never, but I like it. Will you show me how to do it?"

I finish the knot and show him a little trick. I curl the pink square around the black skull-and-bones square, then put them in his breast pocket.

He stands back. So does Grace. Peter looks at himself in the mirror. He turns to the left and to the right and makes an appraisal. He pulls on the wings of the tie and plays with the silk in his breast pocket. Rock 'n' roll.

I can tell he sees his own potential. The change in Peter is evident. Grace grabs my arm and whispers in my ear so the spell won't be broken, "He looks perfect."

He practises tying the knot twice, and then I send them to the cash register and plan my getaway. I don't want to be around when the man at the till asks who helped them out today. I grab my bag and look for the escalator out of the men's section. When I hit the street, my hands are shaking. I am filled with adrenalin. Did I have too much coffee? Is this what going undercover feels like? Am I worried I did something wrong? Then I realize this quaking through my body is the rare, soul-shaking experience of immense joy.

Although I didn't quite believe her at the time, Eve Ensler, the woman who wrote *The Vagina Monologues*, once said that when you give the world what you want the most, you save yourself. Goddammit, the Vagina woman is right.

IT WAS A HARD SUMMER. RIGAUD, DESPITE BEING close to Ontario, was primarily francophone. My French was (and still is) poor, yet sometimes I would have to play the role of waiter. I was terrible. With my high school French I could not decipher the broad vernacular of the locals. I was shy and awkward. As if following some genetic directive, I wore the same glasses and my hair had grown into the same front sweep and boxy back style my father wore. I was scrawny. I had zits and the body language of a person who didn't want to be there. Because the dining room was often hot, I would wear short shorts made from my father's cast-off clothes. I can't imagine what the customers must have thought.

I once had to take the order of a hulking biker with a face hacked out of granite and dressed up with a handlebar mustache. He wore a black leather vest and often was the first customer of the day. I tried to take his order but I couldn't understand what he was saying.

"*Aerole, aerole.*" Was that the French word for something on the menu?

"*Est-que tu peux répéter?*"

"*Aerole, aerole.*" But I could not understand him. I went inside the kitchen to fetch my father.

When he returned he said nothing. He went into the walk-in refrigerator and came back with something he put in a cauldron of hot oil. "What did he say?" My father ignored me. "What did he want?" My father said in a quiet voice, "Egg rolls."

Working for my father was awful, but I took pride in the fact that I was contributing to our family's survival. After the lunch rush I was free to play with Aimee and Lenny. Tammy mostly kept to herself. If it was quiet, we would play the video games, pinball machines, and pool tables in the bar. We would talk with the regulars. Len became their mascot. We also got to know the members of a Journey cover band that had a two-week run at the bar. Their lead singer had stringy brown hair and wore white jeans and a tight tank top just like Steve Perry. I think it was they who drew Tammy out of her shell. Tammy played the guitar and, probably because she was a sixteen-year-old girl, the lead guitarist let her plug in and play through his Marshall stack.

Mostly, we kept our own company. Living in a roadside hotel meant there were no other children around. There were no grassy areas to run through, no swings or seesaws or even a tree to climb, so we made the dusty hotel parking lot our playground. Between the tractor-trailers, trucks, motorcycles, and beaters, we would play tag and hide-and-seek. Instead of the diamond sparkles of dew on grass, we had the gleam of broken bottles and chrome. It was a broken landscape.

In late August my father shut the restaurant down for half a day. He told Tammy and me to watch over Aimee and Lenny, and then he drove off into town. When he returned he was carrying two suitcases, and behind him was my mother. Her hair was shorter, her skin darker than I remembered. She bent down and opened her arms. Aimee and Lenny ran to her. They embraced. My mother cupped my face with her hands. "You're taller," she said.

My mother had returned to the family and that was that. Again, there was no family meeting, no explanation, no perspective. The children were happy, I was happy, yet nothing made sense. I wish I knew how my father was able to draw my mother back in. I had missed her desperately but her absence had been a relief. I knew my father could not bring himself to harm us, and our life in Rigaud, though unhappy, was safer. My mother's return brought back the sick feeling, the fear, back into our family. Would he hurt her again?

He didn't. Whatever powerful emotions had driven him to love my mother as much as hurt her had burned out. The blazing sun was now a black hole. He became detached and dispassionate. He began to drink again, but now it was to dim the present as much as the past. This was the beginning of his real disappearing trick. He was there and not there, a fading presence that was completely swept out of my mind four weeks later when I started grade nine at Hudson High School.

Hudson High was the closest English-language school around. It was ivy-covered and located in the centre of Hudson, one of the wealthiest towns per capita in the province. Attending HHS was like living in a John Hughes film. The Hudson kids would be dropped off in Mercedes and Jaguars. One family used to pull up in a hunter green Land Rover, which, in its WASPy elegance, represented everything I yearned for. The anglophone kids like us who lived outside Hudson and were not wealthy arrived at school on a yellow school bus. The townies called us the "bus kids." But we weren't ostracized or bullied; in fact, Tammy got along fine, but I felt alienated. After my isolation in Sainte-Adèle and the summer of Rigaud, seeing high school girls was a revelation. The Hudson girls were everything my family wasn't: rich, entitled, seemingly happy, perky. How could I not fall in love? There was Megan, who had strawberry-red hair and a button nose. There was a girl named Alison who loved the Cure and had sad, soulful eyes and an aristocratic nose beneath a fringe of blonde bangs. I spoke to them but I never dared to ask them out. I had nothing to offer. If my father had fallen so low, so outside of what I thought was good and right, then what was I? His son. It was a long year.

� hanger symbol�

In the spring of 1984, my father would, from time to time, close the restaurant, put on a blue suit I didn't know he still possessed, and go job hunting in Montreal. Another school

year ended, and again my father had another announcement: he had landed a job as the food and beverage manager
at a tony hotel, the Château Champlain. I was torn over this
development. I considered the possibility he would fall back
into his old late-night habits, that everything that happened
before would happen again. And yet we were returning to
Saint-Lambert, and I to Chambly County High School.

Between leaving Rigaud and moving into our new apartment back in Saint-Lambert, we spent a few weeks at my
grandparents' farm. My grandfather had bought the plot of
nine acres in Saint-Eustache after selling the Dragon Room
Inn. He grew Chinese vegetables: sui choy, gai lan, and bok
choy. Although it is small, I still think of the farm as a
sprawling estate. It has a river running through the back.
My grandpa kept a spring-fed pond filled with trout. There
was a giant oak in the front, which, according to family
lore, had been split by lightning and was now held together
with a corset of steel bands. The two-storey farmhouse was
crumbling brick and ancient. It had a gambrel roof covered
in aluminum and dormers looking north and south. An
entire wing was closed off to everyone and still I have no
idea what lurked there. On the second floor were four bedrooms and two hallway storage closets. It was a far better
place to play hide-and-seek than the parking lot in Rigaud.
The closet on the left stowed the overcoats, wedding dresses,
and other old clothes no one wore anymore. I rummaged
through it with hopes of finding Aimee or Lenny tucked in
between the layers of fabric. Instead I found a suit.

It wasn't a real zoot suit, but it had all the right proportions. Even on the hanger, I could see how I would look in

it. It was a brown double-breasted with purple and grey pencil stripes. It had peak lapels, as all double-breasted suits do, but these lapels were wide, assertive – no, aggressive. Even wider than anything I had seen my father wear in the past. And because of all that had happened over the last fifteen months since that March night, something clicked inside me.

With this suit I would correct all that had gone wrong. I would wear this suit and I would not be shy. I did not understand the mechanism of its appeal, but I saw instinctively in its dimensions, in the way it was a misfit, how it could harness the power of what it means to be a man. Yet I suddenly grasped that I didn't have to be the man my father was. This suit was my way out. I see now that I held up a funhouse mirror to my father and mockingly reflected back to him what he had created, but in that moment, standing in the hall, the suit spiralling in my imagination, I was in the midst of an act of self-creation. I would shave half my head. I would wear the suit with a yellow and black checkered shirt and a studded black leather belt I would loop around my waist three times. It sounds crazy but, trust me, it made perfect sense. I would transform myself, not to emulate my father, but to become my own man. I would not live in his shadow. I would cast my own. I was ready to go back to my old high school, and when I got there, I was going to make one hell of an impression.

IN 1882 OSCAR WILDE TRIED HIS BEST TO OVER-throw a tyrant whose reign would span the last half of the nineteenth century and eventually bleed into the twentieth. It was not Nicholas I of Montenegro, nor was it Franz Joseph I of the Austro-Hungarian Empire. Queen Victoria ruled from 1837 to 1901, but Wilde's goal was not to supplant her. No, Wilde wished to revolt against the dominance and singular plainness of men's dark coats and their equally constrictive consort – pants.

The idea of a suit combination – where a jacket was paired with britches, knee-length breeches, and, later, those familiar long pants – emerged under the influence of, as mentioned, Beau Brummell and neo-classicism. The look was the result of a long evolution that brought greater distinction between masculine and feminine styles of dress. While fashionable men from time to time fell into irrepressible flamboyance (Charles II's friends and the Peacock Revolution of 1960s London are good examples), menswear in Wilde's time had generally flowed with the stronger current of stone-cold simplicity and sobriety. The mood among Wilde's contemporaries to eschew colour and frivolity was later coined the Great Masculine Renunciation by the psychoanalyst John Carl Flügel in 1932. Flügel described the change as "one of the most remarkable events in the whole history of dress, one under the influence of which we are still living, one, moreover, which has attracted far less attention than it deserves: men gave up their right to all the brighter, gayer, more elaborate, and more varied forms of ornamentation, leaving these entirely to the use of women, and thereby making their own tailoring the most austere and ascetic of the arts. Sartorially, this event has surely the right to be considered as 'The Great Masculine Renunciation.' Man abandoned his claim to be beautiful."

The nineteenth century was the century of the plain dark coat. It came in the form of the frock coat, a long coat with a waist seam and hems skirting down low, sometimes to the knees. Depending on fashion the waisting would tighten and loosen through the decades, but one detail remained consistent: the frock coat fell over the body like a shroud of black. The upper class and its imitators, the middle class and the nouveau riche, adopted it as the daytime uniform. Without one, a gentleman could not call on friends. Etiquette guides declared it "indispensable."

With the advent of photography, the visual record between 1840 and the First World War shows the coats were everywhere. Contemporary portraits taken by yeoman photographers in studios in Madison, Wisconsin, and by masters such as Nadar in Paris show that when men needed to dress up, they wore black and shades close to it. Poet Charles Baudelaire celebrated its melancholic ubiquity: "The dress-coat and the frock-coat not only possess their political beauty, which is an expression of universal equality, but also their poetic beauty, which is an expression of the public soul – an immense cortege of undertaker's mutes. . . ."

Oscar Wilde, however, found the dark matte frock coat and the newer dress coat, featuring a cutaway at the front to expose more of the legs, "dull and tedious and depressing in itself, and makes the aspect of club-life and men's dinners monotonous and uninteresting." He wanted to replace it with what he called the "coming garb." Wilde's campaign to reform men's fashion involved a transatlantic stratagem. He embarked on a lecture tour through North America to expound on the topic of the Renaissance, but his under-lying motive was to introduce a new concept and practice of universal beauty, which included clothes.

When he landed in New York in January 1882, he instructed one of the city's tailors to make him a coat "the shade of a lake glistening in the moonlight." Wilde designated the hue "couleur du lac au clair de la lune." He also ordered a tight black velvet doublet. Wilde wanted the sleeves embroidered with flowers and they were to be capped, making them puffy at the shoul-ders. Wilde threw in ruffles and frills for good measure.

While some accounts in the English press, who tracked Wilde's every movement in America, reported some of his lectures as poorly attended, there can be no doubt they took on the status of a cult event. In his first American lecture, in New York's Chickering Hall, the majority of the crowd who

came to see him were dressed in formal evening wear. A few in the audience were described as "pallid" and having "banged hair." Wilde dressed to make his point: "His long hair fell on his shoulders, just showing the lobes of two handsome ears. He wore a dress-coat [whether *couleur du lac* or black, the report does not say], a white silk waistcoat, in which was thrust a white silk handkerchief. A large stud ornamented his shirt bosom. . . . His nether garments did not extend to his ankles, as those of modest men ought to do but stopped at his knees. In fact he wore breeches. They were wavy and loose. . . . He wore pumps [most certainly with the silver buckles], and his black silk stockings extended to his knees, showing a handsome and well-formed calf."

OSCAR WILDE LED THE REVOLT AGAINST THE "DULL AND TEDIOUS" PLAINNESS OF MEN'S CLOTHES.

When he was done, he was applauded wildly and was called upon to do the impossible in a lecture, provide an encore.

By the time Wilde reached Boston, the students at Harvard were ready for him. Up to sixty undergraduates appeared dressed like Wilde, in breeches, stockings, and long curly locks. Judging from the Harvard student press, it was imitation as a form of flattery. In Rochester, the students were so boisterous police arrested one man. Oscar Wilde apostles became a regular feature of nearly every college town on his tour (though in some campuses, the students dressed to mock the man).

While his performances indeed received favourable reviews, Wilde also garnered brickbats. The *Decatur Daily Republican* called him an "aesthetic bundle of egotism from England . . . who has an unmistakable and vulgar greed for American dollars." It also made sly references to his effeminate appearance and sexuality:

> Oscah, Oscah,
> You little pet
> You look so la-de-dah
> In your suit of velvet jet;
> It grieves the girl art student
> That she must say ta-ta,
> For the darling of the aesthetes
> Is this renowned Oscah!

In the face of sometimes withering press, Wilde did his best to carry on. In Racine, Wisconsin, he finally broke down and claimed he could not read his manuscript due to exhaustion. However, by the time he reached Colorado Springs in April 1882, he had memorized his talks. While the English press continued to ridicule both his dress and the tour ("Oscar Wilde, in satin knee-breeches, talks vast nonsense and takes a fortune from American dupes"), in fact, he wore his breeches less and less often.

When he finally returned from America, Wilde prepared and presented a new lecture for London, entitled "Impressions of America." For the talk, he wore a standard black cutaway coat with tails and standard black pants. Perhaps the Americans and their reputed artless penchant for common sense had a greater effect on him than he had on them: "The first thing that struck me on landing in America was that if the Americans are not the most well-dressed people in the world, they are the most comfortably dressed."

From then on reports would continue to crop up regarding Wilde's dress. One observer noted the lack of affectation and praised him for his athletic frame. When his fame as a dress and aesthetic reformer was finally eclipsed by his fame as a dramatist, a reporter dared to ask Wilde why he no longer wore his trademark costume. Wilde answered he was no longer a lecturer on Aestheticism but a successful playwright.

Ironically, despite all the barbs he received in America, Wilde did spur a fad for short pants: "Bicyclists, hunting men, tennis players, and a few of the younger sons of fond mamas took eagerly to knickerbockers, and displayed them on every possible occasion." Breeches never made a full return in formal and polite company, but evening shirt fronts became "ribbed, fluted and decorated in various ways." Elaborate waistcoats and vests also became popular again. And when you don a pair of trousers with a broad satin stripe on the side and a dinner jacket with shiny lapels or a fully embroidered smoking jacket for a black-tie event, you can thank Wilde for his part in the struggle against the dull and the tedious.

"LET ME DO THAT FOR YOU."

Bill is trying to stoop down to hem the pants of a customer who is sixty years younger than he is. It doesn't seem right, but he waves me off.

"Then let me get you a chair."

"No, no," says Bill. Part of the tailor's code is to maintain the dignity of the client. Tailors already force their customers to disrobe and subject themselves to scrutiny in the search for physical defects ("Left shoulder drops half an inch," whispers the tailor to his apprentice taking notes). It's a point of professional pride to limit any further loss of face. Obliging the young man to stand upon the chair, it appears, would be a violation of tact. Bill, on his knees, nearly prostrate, pins the pant hems so the legs have only the smallest break and then slowly unfolds himself as he rises. Once up, he declares, "Okay, there you go."

Bill sends the man back into the changing room. When the curtain closes, my master tailor smiles at me. He swipes forward a few strands of his thinning hair and adjusts his glasses.

Bill is getting old, and his family wants him to retire. His younger brother, Milton, a financier and philanthropist, has recently purchased the building in which their father originally founded the business. The original Modernize occupied the entire ground floor of the heritage building across the street from the current shop. It has four storeys of windows – but the building actually includes a fifth cheater floor. (It's called a cheater because it shares the double-height windows on the fourth storey, a design that saves the owner 20 percent on property tax.)

Bill says Milton's plan is to have Bill live on one of the upper floors of the building in a newly created condo apartment with his wife, Zoe. Apparently, their rambling bungalow is in a state of disrepair. Another part of Milton's plan is to open a smaller tailoring studio on the ground floor, one that would be a closet compared with the space we're in now. The expectation is that Bill would dramatically scale back on his workload.

Bill is excited to return to the old site. Though he has occupied the current store for more than half a century, he sees the return to the old shop as a way of honouring his father. "It's just like going home," Bill says. "My father was there. Now, I'll be there. Who would have thought we would be there a hundred years after my father started Modernize?"

I know Jack relishes the idea of retirement. Every summer he dashes off to Europe on a tour of Michelin-starred restaurants. He would enjoy a release from his labours, but he won't quit unless Bill does because they are old-school

Chinese. Jack will follow his older brother. Bill, however, acts oblivious to the idea of retirement.

I'm quietly grateful. Everything Milton has done is motivated by love and concern for his older brothers, but Bill shouldn't retire. I believe he would fade and die without the routine of the shop. It gives him structure and contact with new people every day. It keeps him young and spry. Okay, maybe he shouldn't be bending down on his knees to fix pant hems anymore, but to my mind this all points to my indispensability. If there was ever a place where I am actually needed, it's here at the shop. Isn't it?

And I need Bill. If he quits, I'm in trouble. I've only just begun to learn how to sew. I thought a year would be all it would take for me to get the swing of things, enough that I could work at the shop full-time and make a living. I know now I'll never be able to make coats the way a pro like Park does, one every two days without fail. But I think I can make a great pair of jeans. I really do.

For the last several weeks, I've taken a stab at making a few on my own. For my current pair, I bought purple-black denim with tiny slubs. And the continuous practice of starting and stopping the straight stitcher has paid off. Okay, I can't make welt pockets or hip pockets or lining or vents, or attach sleeves to a discerning customer's satisfaction. Luckily for me, jeans have none of those things. They have been far easier to make than my father's suit has been to alter. I'm not hung up on thinking that I'm doing irreparable damage. No one at the shop can tell me I'm doing it wrong. And, to be frank, I may not be the best sewer in the world but – and I tell you this as a fashion critic and a trained designer – I cut a mean pair of pants. They look awesome. The pants are narrow in the thighs and calves. I've cut them short to show off a bit of sock. The seat is flattering and on the back pocket, where Levi Strauss & Co. of San Francisco put their famous arcuate topstitching (that double line of gold that looks like a seagull), I've put a cursive JJ.

I recently wore a prototype on a trip to New York. I was having breakfast at an eatery on Madison Avenue and 82nd while waiting for the Metropolitan Museum to open when I noticed three women in a booth staring at me. A leonine brunette leaned towards me.

"Are you a fashion designer?" She wore a pencil skirt suit and had full lips that said "Welcome to the Upper East Side."

"No, I'm not from New York."

She made a face of disappointment. "Sorry, I thought you might be Thakoon Panichgul." This was a flattering case of mistaken identity. Panichgul is one of New York's hottest young fashion designers.

"But I am an apprentice tailor," I said, offering hope.

"What do you do?"

I could have told her I was learning the basics and that I spend most of my days straight-stitching grids, but here I was in New York, where you can be anything you say you are. And so I could have told her I was a master stylist in charge of all the young clientele who came to our esteemed shop, which would have been true, but somehow off the mark. What I wanted to tell her was that I had learned how to make a wicked pair of jeans. I needed someone to believe I was actually learning the trade and accomplishing something at the shop. That I was not returning home every night empty-handed. So, I stood, lifted my Donegal tweed sports coat, and pirouetted.

"I made these."

They gasped.

"Do you make women's jeans?" asked the second woman. Then the third, a beautiful blonde whose skin and hair seemed kissed by a Nebraskan sun, leaned across their table towards me, parting her two friends, and said breathlessly, "I'm the size six fit model for Ralph Lauren."

I took a seat next to them and, while I finished my fruit salad, I told them about Bill and Modernize. I told them about my hopes.

"You should make jeans," said Miss Nebraska. "Women will pay anything for jeans that really fit them." By the time I ordered my third cup of coffee, they had convinced me all I had to do was get Bill to see that jeans are the way of the future. My future.

The whole subject of jeans needs reckoning with at the shop. Bill can't just close the door to the idea. Even though younger customers have been coming to order suits, they often ask Bill to reduce the rise of the pants so that they sit on the hip bone instead of across the natural waistline in line with the belly button. In other words, men want their suit pants to feel like a pair of jeans.

I'm not saying Bill should just accept my idea because everyone wears jeans now. I understand jeans have a long history of appalling people and can still cause a ruckus. For example, in 2010 a Memphis man by the name of Kenneth E. Bonds allegedly shot an adolescent boy in the buttock because of how he wore his jeans. Bonds ordered the teen and his friends, all perfect strangers to the accused, to pull their pants up. They refused and an argument ensued. Then Bonds pulled out a semi-automatic pistol and began firing at the fleeing teens. One took a bullet in the rear cheek.

The teens had been wearing their pants in a manner known as sagging. Sagging involves pulling pants (almost always jeans) far below the waist to reveal some underwear. A number of towns and cities in the United States have attempted to outlaw the practice, claiming it is indecent. In one case that made its way through the New York courts, a police officer ticketed a man and scribbled in his citation: "Pants [are pulled] down below his buttocks exposing underwear and potentially showing private parts." The man was charged with disorderly conduct but found not guilty. In his decision, the judge ruled that wearing saggy pants hanging from your thighs might be ridiculous, but it is not illegal. He reasoned, "While most of us may consider it distasteful, and indeed foolish, to wear one's pants so low as to expose the underwear . . . people can dress as they please, wear anything, so long as they do not offend public order and decency." The judge went further by asserting the U.S. Constitution protects the right of Americans to be foolish as they choose to be. You have to love the First Amendment.

The popularity of sagging has to be put at the low-hanging crotch, at least partly, of actor and former singer Mark Wahlberg, the erstwhile Marky Mark. In 1992, Wahlberg appeared in a notorious series of advertisements for Calvin Klein, often wearing nothing more than the designer's underwear. He also appeared in Calvin Klein jeans sagged to reveal perfectly cut abdomen muscles, a good portion of his pelvis, and, most importantly, the branded waistband of the underwear. Suburban teens soon followed Wahlberg's impressively hypersexual example. Now, twenty years later, surfers, skateboarders, indie rockers, it doesn't matter, they all sag — and we know, thanks to Marky Mark, what brands of underwear teen boys wear without ever having to ask.

It's not only jeans. Forty years before Wahlberg, the provocative deployment of pants helped another man achieve notoriety. This is how country singer Bob Luman recalled a young Elvis Presley taking the stage at a high school dance in Kilgore, Texas: "This cat came out wearing red pants and a green coat and a pink shirt and socks. . . . Then he hit his guitar a lick, and he broke two strings . . . and he hadn't done anything yet, and these high school girls were screaming and fainting . . . and then he started to move his hips real slow."

One may wonder if the erotic quality of pants is impossible to quell. It seems any aspect of them, in whole or in part, can lead to pandemonium. One reason is so obvious it may escape notice: the garment covers the genitals and anus. Loose or tight, pants can spell trouble. The fitted, plain-front pants of the 1960s and 1970s provided, as fashion historian Farid Chenoune described, an "exposed-beam" look (think of Andy Warhol's cover for the Rolling Stones' album *Sticky Fingers*, featuring a working zipper on a close-up photograph of a male crotch in tight jeans). A decade later the revealing fronts were superseded by loose multi-pleated pants by Armani (again!), Gianni Versace, and France's Marithé + Francois Girbaud. Sprouting four or more tucks on each side of the fly, the pants effectively buried the penis in folds of fabric. Even so the sexual emphasis simply shifted to the backside where the seat was very tight.

But pants, like lapels, aren't all about sex. During the upheavals of the French Revolution, knee-breeches-wearing aristocrats used to refer to the *pantalon*-wearing shopkeepers and artisans of Paris as *sans-culottes*, the people who didn't wear breeches. It was meant to be a put-down, but the *sans-culottes* moniker was proudly taken up by working-class demonstrators and barricade-builders who would become the volunteer ranks of the National Guard and the Revolutionary army.

James Fennell, an English writer who witnessed the events taking place in Paris at the time, observed how pants and breeches played a strange side role in the drama. He reports in the summer of 1792 how a mob flooded into the royal chambers of Louis XVI. A butcher by the name of Legendre

soon arrived with a group of his friends; one of them presented to the King a red cap; one of the grenadiers [who protected the King] put it aside with his hand, and was wounded in the arm by the thrust of a pike. Another man approached, offered to the King a bottle, and desired him to drink to the health of the nation. Someone offered to fetch a glass; the King refused the offer; and immediately, without fear, and without repugnance, he applied the impure vessel to his august lips, and drank of the uncertain liquor. One of the grenadiers asked, as a favour, the honour of drinking after his master; he was worthy of obtaining it, and it was granted: taking advantage of this moment of confusion, one of the rabble placed himself the red cap upon the head of the King.

[225]

Then the King was sat on a stool and lifted into the mob. Fennell watched as the crowd become frenzied and began breaking into all parts of the palace. On the roof a gang became "employed in erecting a pole, from which was suspended a pair of breeches." Later the crowd cheered themselves, *"Vivent les sans-culottes!"*

So, as you can see, jeans and pants do have a history of causing trouble. But if I make my case carefully to Bill and show him the upside of Modernize making jeans on the side, I think he will come over to my point of view. For some reason I have a real knack for making jeans, and this way I can actually earn a wage. Which I would argue is the point of being a tailor.

Besides, what's the harm in asking?

WHEN MY FAMILY MOVED BACK TO SAINT-LAMBERT in the autumn of 1984, my father was a changed man. I assume it was guilt that made his hair continue to thin and guilt that made his body not so much soften as collapse into itself. He could have sought forgiveness, but he never apologized to anyone. Instead he became remote. Remorse and shame had muted him.

My father had once been the centre around which our family's life revolved, even if he was often absent from home. With my mother's unexpected return to the family, the children temporarily reorganized their orbits around her. But once we returned to Saint-Lambert, whatever gravitational field had held us together finally weakened, as each of us adopted our own careening, elliptical path. I spent very little time with my family and knew next to nothing of what was going on in their lives. What I knew for certain, though, was that my father was no longer violent to my mother; in fact, they hardly spoke to each other. He had lost his aggression, as well as his arrogance, vitality, vigour, and whatever it was that had made him both dangerous and attractive. He had become a ghost.

With the new job at the hotel he was able to revive his suit-wearing ways, but he took no pleasure in the way he dressed. The cufflinks and waggish double-breasted chalk stripes were replaced by a trio of sober blue suits that fit him well enough, but they were off-the-rack affairs. They were bland. My father did his best to avoid drinking whiskey, and there were no drunken binges for the next two years. Nor were there any congratulations or encouragement for his relative sobriety. My father was not on a twelve-step program – his alcoholism continued to be unacknowledged. He could have benefited from support from someone, anyone – even his troublesome boy. But it was too late for the two of us.

I seized on my return to Chambly County High School as an opportunity to lose myself in others. I joined the volleyball team and the drama club. I started singing and collaborating with classmates on comic books. In September, I made my sartorial debut with my grandfather's suit. In October, I kissed a girl for the first time. By December, I had fallen in love. My father was beside the point. I ignored him. And even though his schedule allowed him to come home for supper and to stay in for the evening, his presence in our family had permanently shrunk. He was there but I no longer needed him. He would come home and drink cheap red wine until he fell asleep. When I got home at night from rehearsal or volleyball practice, I would find him asleep on the living room couch.

I believe the dark moods that gripped my father began

then to take hold of me. I suppose that today my condition might be diagnosed as depression or a side effect of attention deficit disorder, but it manifested itself as juvenile melancholy. I wrote poetry and learned to play tuneless songs on my sister's guitar. I kept verse and lyrics in numbered pink and yellow Hilroy exercise books and took midnight strolls. I became Byronesque but not sickly. I was still short compared with my friends, but I could jump high enough to grab a basketball hoop. My body had become lean and I was strong. My waist measured twenty-eight inches. My father had eight inches over me in the belly. When I looked at him I saw how he kept all of his failings there.

∆

The summer after I graduated from high school, I got a job at Tarte Julie as a kitchen helper. My previous experience in my father's restaurant ill prepared me to work in a properly run outfit but I caught on. I worked late, spent my money on comic books and movies, and wondered what college would bring. On my days off, my friend Adrien and I started sparring with two pairs of old boxing gloves. We spent a good part of August pounding the shit out of each other. It's funny how being punched in the head can actually be a welcome diversion when you are young.

One day Adrien left the gloves in my bedroom. My father came home early as was his new habit, but this time he was hammered. Relapsed into the old pattern, he barged into my room, filling the space with the sickly, smoky smell of whiskey. It made me hostile and alert. Then he saw the leather gloves. His voice slurred, "Do you want to box?"

I made a quick calculation. Despite his physical decline my father still had thicker arms and broader shoulders than I did. He weighed 160 pounds, more than Sugar Ray Leonard. He might still be strong, but he was also slow.

The light of the late summer evening flooded into my room. We cleared a space and began. He landed some heavy punches on my ribs. I pushed him back and jabbed him with my left hand. To his surprise and mine, his head snapped back twice, then three times. He padded around and then lunged at me. I pushed him away. He came forward again and we clinched.

I wonder now what would have happened if I had just held him at that moment. Just wrapped my hands around him, slipped the gloves off, and hugged him, bearing his weight. I would have felt the sweat on his cheek and smelled the booze sharply on his breath, but I no longer feared him or what he could do. I would have felt his heart beating madly, and I would have felt mine beating too. He wouldn't have been too heavy for me to bear.

I could have said, "Come on, Pa, sit down. You've been drinking." Instead I jabbed hard with my left and hooked with my right and caught him on the temple. He straightened up. I began to sting him in the forehead. He staggered back with a crash, his body slamming the bedroom door shut. Knockout. I smiled when it happened but really I wanted to cry. I took my gloves off, but I couldn't get out. He was blocking the way. So I dragged him by his feet to the middle of the room and left him sprawled there on the floor. Then I climbed over his body and shut the door behind me.

HE WAS BORN IN 1894. HIS PARENTS NAMED HIM Edward Albert Christian George Andrew Patrick David. His family would call him by the last of his Christian names, David. But the world knew him as Edward, Prince of Wales, later Edward VIII, the King of England, and, after he abdicated, the Duke of Windsor. It was he who became the most fashionable man in the world. Edward's influence on menswear remains wide-ranging and profound, and today no man can dress in a suit without touching something he transformed with his unique sense of style.

In Edward's memoir, he describes the time of his birth as the golden hour of Britain's upper class. His great-grandmother was Queen Victoria. His grandfather and namesake was the heir to the throne. His father, George, was second in succession. As a boy he asked his grandfather, "Who will be greater, God or great-grandmama?" When his grandfather answered, "God, of course, my boy," the princeling could only say, "Great-grandmama won't like that, will she?"

Edward remembered his grandfather, who became King Edward VII, as "the last Englishman to have an uninterruptedly good time." Historians and royal watchers agree it was from his grandfather that the younger Edward inherited his knack for dressing well.

The older Edward's fashion record is itself impressive. As a boy, Edward VII, called Bertie by his family, had worried his parents, Queen Victoria and Albert, Prince Consort. Bertie was known for throwing tantrums and spat at people who annoyed him. More than once, he clubbed tutors with his walking stick. Eventually, he outgrew his social clumsiness and began to build a reputation as a clotheshorse. At seventeen he was shipped off to live at a villa called White Lodge on the outskirts of London. Assigned to him to serve as role models and companions were three men in their twenties. Two were majors who had been awarded the Victoria Cross for acts of bravery in the Crimean War. All were reminded of what was expected of them in a letter written by his mother, but most likely drafted by his father:

> Dress is a trifling matter which might not be raised to too much importance in our own eyes. But it gives also the one outward sign from which people in general can and often do judge upon the inward state of mind and feeling of a person; for this they all see, while the other they cannot see. On that account it is of some importance particularly in persons of high rank. I must now say that we do not wish to control your own tastes and fancies, which, on the contrary, we wish you to indulge and develop, but we do expect that you will never wear anything extravagant or

slang, not because we don't like it but because it would prove a want of self-respect and be an offence against decency, leading, as it has often done before in others, to an indifference to what is morally wrong.

A few years later, Bertie's father wrote to remind him to "borrow nothing from the groom or the gamekeeper."

The warnings failed. Though his parents strived to turn him into "the repository of all the intellectual and moral qualities by which the state is held together and under the guidance of which it advances in the great path of civilization," they never felt he could fulfil his role as future monarch. He was sidelined from the business of the Empire and thereby gained a "social sovereignty." So freed, he became a regular customer of the Moulin Rouge in Paris, where dancers would greet him with an informal, "Ullo, Wales." Bertie also became bolder with his dress, adopting a more casual approach to clothes. He took pleasure in loud tweeds and checks (a look borrowed from the groom and the gamekeeper) and popularized creased pants, though his creases were on the sides and not in the front as they are today. He brought the Homburg hat (similar to a fedora except its brim is turned up) to the English-speaking world on his return from a trip to Germany. Of course, it was he who made leaving the bottom button of a jacket undone de rigueur, stemming from his growing royal belly requiring relief, and to this day even the thinnest man should remember to do this. And it was as far back as the 1860s that Bertie sent the lounge suit – the type of suit we are most familiar with today – down the long road to respectability. Before Bertie, the lounge suit was considered a form of country clothes to be worn during such sporting activities as shooting. It was Bertie who brought the lounge suit to the city.

The younger Edward had fond memories of his Grandpapa Bertie. On his eighth birthday, Edward received from this larger-than-life patriarch a bicycle and a giant knife. Edward's father protested, saying it was too dangerous a gift. Edward VII scoffed, "Nonsense, George, I've never heard of a boy without a knife."

When his grandfather died, Edward's father became King George V, who would rule the British Empire for twenty-six years. It was a setback for men's style. The new King was conservative in manner and belief, and he extinguished, in Edward's words, "the light-hearted cosmopolitan" sparkle of court life. George was a stickler for formality. Having a family dinner with George V meant Edward had to dress in white tie and tails and pin the Garter Star – an eight-pointed medal of the knightly Order of the Garter – over his left breast. The popularity of the lounge suit regressed under George V, who preferred and insisted upon the longer frock coat. It didn't stop there. He was also an enemy of the bowler, which, following the long historical trend of menswear becoming more casual with each passing era, had made its way from the heads of sporting aristocracy to the urban working and middle classes. It was another hat Bertie had been known to wear, but George called it "rat-catcher fashion." It was as if the son were trying to undo all of the father's innovations.

George V was also, as the knife story suggests, a fretful father. All through his son's childhood, he obsessed over the prince's size and recorded his son's weight in a diary. He would chastise the boy for not learning to ride a horse well enough and then, after his son had mastered the skill and pursued it with gusto, he would chastise him for riding too much.

They did have their tender moments. When George V took Edward by train off to naval college, the young prince was in tears. On the journey there, Edward listened to his father's stories about life in the navy. Anything to reassure the boy. As they arrived at the Royal Naval College, Osborne on the Isle of Wight, his father said, "Now that you are leaving home, and going out into the world, always remember I am your best friend." Life at Osborne was hard for Edward. Prior to it his only company had been his siblings. Adjusting to life at school proved too daunting. In his first year, he ranked thirtieth in History, fifty-seventh in Navigation, and fifty-ninth in Engineering in his class of fifty-nine shipmates. He fared no better at Oxford.

Then the First World War erupted. He begged his father to allow him to enlist. George V relented, though the King made him promise that under no circumstances would he enter battle or travel roads on the front alone. Once with the British Expeditionary Force in France, Edward was kept busy with make-work, ferrying dispatches between generals. Eventually, he did come close to the front and had a first-hand view of the carnage, but he never fired a shot. Veterans of the war remembered Edward best as the Prince who rode a bicycle between headquarters, carrying on the business of a staff officer. He was not a distinguished soldier, certainly not a hero. Yet he had seen the world in a way his father never would. When he returned to civilian life in 1919, he was twenty-five years old. The years in France had freed him from his constrained life under his father's influence, and he was ready to make his mark.

Young Edward's fashion sense owed much to Bertie, but it was also informed by his own feel for the times. In his memoirs, Edward describes how the Russian Revolution, his awareness of the growing disenchantment taking hold in postwar England, and his own demobilization all influenced his approach to fashion. In particular, Edward recalls an incident when his father was asked by the War Office to review a parade of fifteen thousand disabled and discharged veterans as they marched in Hyde Park. As his father inspected the front line of men parading in divisions but dressed in civilian clothes, a "commotion" broke out when a veteran unfurling a banner cried out, "Where is this land fit for heroes?" The King was then surrounded by the veterans. No harm was meant – all they wanted was to shake the sovereign's hand – but the fracas led the King to say to Edward, "Those men were in a funny temper." It was clear to Edward his father was out of touch with his people.

One of the earliest initiatives Edward took on the fashion front was to shepherd the bowler back into the royal sartorial lexicon by wearing it on official functions. The King saw a press photo of the offence, possibly the one where Edward is inspecting the dire conditions in a London slum, and called his son to "the carpet." Edward recounts the conversation:

> Now I would just as soon have gone around wearing a gold crown as a shiny top hat; and in defending my attitude I maintained that far from showing disrespect to the city fathers, or letting down my "position," my reluctance to

wear a silk hat did in fact exhibit a certain sagacity in what we nowadays call public relations. My point was that since the political cartoonists had, rightly or wrongly, made the top hat a universal symbol of the bloated, predatory capitalist, the male members of the royal family would be well advised not to wear one during times of social tension.

Edward was right. He understood how his clothes could be coded and read, how every detail was under scrutiny, and how he could turn this scrutiny to his and his family's advantage. He became a fashion star with the goal of reviving the royal family's public image. But don't make the mistake of thinking he was an early version of a fashionista. In historical influence, he dwarfs such recent style icons as footballer David Beckham (white athletes with shaved heads); actors George Clooney (who suggested the simply notched tuxedo jacket could look nearly as good as the peaked lapel), Richard Gere (Armani-bringer), and Hugh Grant (ambassador of the spread-collared shirt); and musical performers Sean "Diddy" Combs, Kanye West, and André Benjamin (all of whom revived black dandyism). Only perhaps Ralph Lauren's liberation of both English and preppy style from a white, Anglo-Saxon Protestant establishment can rival the way the Prince of Wales transformed men's ideas of how to dress.

Edward's sartorial influence was not limited to the British Isles. Starting in 1919, he began a long transatlantic relationship with America with the aim of improving Anglo-American relations and showcasing English menswear. The hope was he could increase the demand for uniquely British, Scottish, and Irish textiles, shirts, hats, shoes, and, yes, suits.

It worked. H.L. Mencken, the American satirist, wrote in the aftermath of a 1924 tour: "The Prince of Wales, in his recent sojourn in these parts, left a trail of woe and misery behind him. Think of the agonized fate of the young men who will be husbands of the girls he favored with his fleeting attention! Think of the years and years that the poor bimbos [he means the men] will have to listen to politely disparaging comparisons of themselves with this *beau idéal* of their ladies!"

In 1924, arriving at the Meadow Brook Country Club on Long Island to play polo, Edward surprised the members by wearing brown suede shoes with a grey double-breasted suit. At the time, suede shoes were considered homosexual attire, though they were oxymoronically called "brothel creepers" because of their soft rubber soles. In my mind, he combined the high and the correct (the double-breasted suit) with the low and the scandalous (suede) with aplomb. From then on, wearing suede well with a suit was considered a sign of supreme sophistication. Regarding his double-breasted jacket, despite its sharp, martial silhouette derived from naval uniforms, Edward saw it as another step in the evolution of the casual approach: it dispensed with the need to wear a vest.

The intriguing figure stitching together Edward's effort to relax menswear was Frederick Scholte of Savile Row. Serving Edward from 1919 to 1959, the Dutch immigrant was a most improbable tailor for Edward's project. Scholte was known for his prickly nature and strict ideas regarding male dress. He invented the London Cut, the shape most associated with Savile Row, with built-up shoulders and a nipped waist to create a strong V-shape. His coats had longer skirts or hems, though marginally so, as he always proportioned them to give the illusion of greater stature. As Edward recalls, Scholte disliked "any form of exaggeration in the style of the coat." He refused to make clothes for stage or screen. He even turned down Fred Astaire. Only twice did he acquiesce and make suits for actors with the understanding they would never wear his masterworks during a performance.

In New York, a 1998 Sotheby's auction and 2002 exhibition at the Costume Institute at the Metropolitan Museum of Art provided the opportunity to reappraise Edward's influence and take a closer look at Scholte's work. What emerged was the Prince's deep understanding of the role of the media and how his clothes interacted with it. For example, as one *New York Times* reporter noted, Edward had "evening suits from midnight-blue wool instead of black. The details in a blue suit, he reasoned, registered more crisply in strobe-light photographs." One could imagine how his taste for tartans also shared a similar graphic punch even before the widespread use of colour photography. One suit at the auction was a red tartan made in 1897, possibly for his father. It was then altered for Edward and may have been the spark behind a plaid (like tartan but with no clan affiliation) dinner jacket fad in the 1950s. But there were some important caveats for the men who would wear it. *Life*, the same magazine that published his memoirs during this period and included many compelling images of Edward in his sartorial glory, made sure to remind all that only the host should wear a plaid dinner jacket. For a final word on Edward's love of tartan, former *Vogue* editor Diana Vreeland once said that the "Duke of Windsor had style in every buckle on his kilt, every check of his country suits."

Some of Edward's innovations were more subtle. Inspection of his suits on auction and at exhibition confirmed he was an early adopter of belted pants. He disliked suspenders. He also preferred zippers to buttoned flies. These were minor details, but they had the effect of simplifying the construction of pants, which led to lowered waistlines and reduced bulk in the front. He also popularized the cuffing of pants – with their added weight, pant cuffs help maintain a straight long line without any breaks in the leg, which is the right choice for a shorter man wearing the full-legged pants that Edward favoured.

The list could go on. Every man who has worn a striped tie and yet never belonged to an exclusive club or an army regiment does so because Edward, who was a Grenadier Guard and thus permitted to wear its blue-and-red design, made the stripes so attractive. If he pulls on a Fair Isle sweater, he has Edward to thank for inspiring a love of intricate geometric patterns on the front. And the turn-down collar, so comfortable, so flattering to the face? Edward VIII, the Duke of Windsor. Fashion superstar.

Of course, trying to pinpoint how Edward was able to summon all these elements into a style that is nothing short of compelling is difficult.

My trip to New York was a pilgrimage to the Costume Institute to see for myself what his clothes might reveal. In

a cluttered office in the bowels of the Metropolitan Museum
of Art, a fine-boned man with blond hair shook my hand.
It was Andrew Bolton, curator of the Costume Institute. We
put on white gloves and, after continuing deeper into the
basement, we opened a metal door and came to a high-
ceilinged room illuminated with neon lights and filled
with massive metal cabinets. One was entirely dedicated to
Edward's clothes. Bolton laid them out on a table. There
was the morning suit Edward wore to marry American
divorcée Wallis Simpson. Its price was abdication and
nearly uninterrupted exile from England. Like a true relic,
the suit was too precious to touch. I asked about the blue
window-pane suit. Bolton gently patted the sleeve. It had
been featured in a spread for *Vogue*. After hearing so much

IN SEEKING FREEDOM AND INFORMALITY, EDWARD VIII, THE DUKE OF
WINDSOR, TRANSFORMED MEN'S IDEAS OF HOW TO DRESS.

about Scholte's rigid ways, it was a shock to see how soft the jacket looked.

"Quite a heavy wool. It's a tweed," said Bolton. "It's a much more relaxed shoulder. And look at this. His left-hand pocket is wider than his right-hand pocket because that's where he kept his cigarette case."

I know now that I expected too much from these suits. I can't recall precisely what I had hoped to find, but I did feel disappointment. They were undeniably well made but not beyond the skills of a conscientious tailor with some vision, the kind one can still find in London, Hong Kong, or New York.

Bolton showed me a double-breasted chalk stripe and another tartan suit. I could see the exquisite pocket details: on one coat the side pocket opening was crescent shaped, and the balance was perfect between the front and the back panels. This allowed the coat to look light. But, again, nothing. It was not that the suits were lifeless; in fact, they were brimming with possibilities. Later, I was reminded of what Richard Jenkyns once wrote about the bowler: "The bowler is effective through its neutrality: it is what you do with it that counts."

Edward used the suit and its undeniable elegance to help close the gap between his family and their nation. Even as he was edged out of official royal life, Edward used clothes the same way Princess Diana used clothes – to bring the royal family more in step with the times and modernize the monarchy.

But it wasn't the clothes that were transformative. It was Edward.

Don't misunderstand me. Clothes do have a semiotic, a meaning in themselves. When I work on my father's clothes, they do speak to me. The suit itself only tells a very short story, and the memories summoned are fragmented, wide oceans of murk whose depths I struggle to fathom.

Edward's clothes, though they trace the shape of a man and remind us of the path he struck through his life, are nevertheless empty. In the same way my father's suit is now empty. Wool, canvas, lint, and silk twist, along with pricks of blood and the oil from my fingertips, it's all there. Yet I still don't have my father, I only have his suit.

You can't have the magic of the suit without the man.

In 1989, MY PARENTS WERE IN A STRANGE DÉTENTE. Aimee and Lenny were now teenagers with lives of their own outside my family's home, and without the anchor of little children, my parents' paths continued to diverge. My mother was working as a waitress at a Chinese restaurant whose owners did not know my father. My father slept on the couch. They never kissed. They never touched. They hardly spoke to each other. I didn't worry there might be violence between them anymore because they no longer had the means to hurt each other. They were in a marriage without love.

Not that I took the time to notice. I was twenty years old and had completed my first two semesters of fine arts school at Concordia University and then spent a semester in France studying painting. When I returned, it was my mother who greeted me alone at the airport. As we walked to the parking lot, she told me she had news.

"I left your father, that's it."

Before I could ask her any questions, she pointed to an old truck I had never seen before. At the wheel was a stranger. "His name is Romeo."

They had met at the restaurant where she worked. Romeo was in his sixties, twenty years older than my mother. He was tall and had a Gallic nose and wore his grey hair swept back. My mother said he worked as a stonemason.

I sat in the jump seat of the unfamiliar four-cylinder pickup truck with my duffle bag on my knees and watched as my mother talked to this stranger with the intimate, nonsensical-to-others domestic prattle of a happy couple.

They brought me to an apartment building I had not noticed before even though it was a few blocks down from our own. Romeo dropped my bag in the front bedroom. I knew Tammy was safely enrolled at the University of Waterloo, a whole province away from this insanity, but where were Aimee and Lenny?

"Your father took them with him."

"Where did he go?"

"He went to Vancouver."

Vancouver. My father had fond memories of the city from the cross-country road trip he made as a teenager, before he married my mother. From time to time throughout my childhood, he would talk about the city with its warmer winters and the smell of the ocean in the air. It was a land of giant cedars and dogwoods, where some of the trees made cracking sounds at night as their bark ripped apart. To get there he had taken the Trans-Canada Highway, which wound its way between mountain peaks and through tunnels before it terminated at a city that hung onto the side of a mountain range. I always imagined with a shrug of the earth Vancouver might slide into the ocean and disappear. It was the farthest away from Montreal you could go and still be in mainland Canada.

That was the end of our family and my sense of having a home in the world. From then on, no matter where I lived, it would always feel impermanent, as if at any moment someone could knock down my tent and tell me to move on. I will admit I was ready to leave home at the time, the way young adults are meant to leave their families behind. But in my case, my family home was swept away before I could let go of it. I had returned from France to find my family no longer existed.

I was not outwardly angry at my mother or her new boyfriend. I feigned indifference. Whatever, right? Wrong. I wanted only to get away from this strange apartment.

I moved in with my girlfriend, Helen. We had been dating for a year. During my time in France we wrote loving letters to each other. We lasted another year together, sharing a room in a house filled with McGill University graduate students who studied agriculture and zoology. The house was an old brick semi-detached in a town called Sainte-Anne-de-Bellevue, which was the home of McGill's experimental farms. I continued my studies at Concordia, which was in downtown Montreal, commuting by train every day. I began to see familiar faces in the cars. I met a dance student named Anya who also lived in Sainte-Anne. She had an alto voice and smooth dark brown hair and one of the saddest life stories I had ever heard. I discovered Anya had a mercurial temper and a bohemian heart. We soon began to meet and sit on the train together. Eventually, I fell in love with her and confessed so to my diary. A suspicious Helen read the entry and cast me out of the house. With the selfish heartlessness of the young, I took my belongings and simply walked a few doors down to Anya's house. By the end of our first week together, I asked her to marry me. By the second week, we had moved into a new place, still in Sainte-Anne, but far enough from Helen that I could walk out the door without fear of bumping into her. Then one night in bed with Anya, I moved my hands lightly over her body. I wanted to make love, but she grabbed my wrist and moved my hand off her. Stung by the rejection, I snapped. I became my father. I went downstairs and started to smash a table with my fists. Anya, rightfully scared and confused, came downstairs and pointed at the door.

"Get out."

"I'm sorry. I don't know what's wrong with me."

"I don't care. I've seen enough abuse in my family. I don't want this shit from you. Get out."

What else could I do? What else did I deserve? I dressed as warmly as I could and I walked along the waterfront of Sainte-Anne for hours in the early morning, facing the horrifying realization that I had absorbed the terrible lessons of my father, that I was more like him than not. I was afraid of myself and stunned by my irrational anger and my sense of entitlement to Anya's body. It was as if I were acting out some forgotten night between my parents. When the sun finally came up and I could no longer walk back and forth along the river, I returned to Anya's place. All my things were piled on the porch. We had lasted a month together.

I was forced to live with my mother and Romeo. I fell into a deep depression. It was the first time I ever felt like killing myself. Luckily, Sean, another childhood friend, heard about my morose behaviour and decided to intervene. With Paquito, he roused me out of my bed and sat me on a stool in front of his father's basement parlour bar, where he mixed me a heavy drink called Corn 'n' Oil, a Barbadian concoction made of lime juice, a liquor called falernum, and blackstrap rum. I don't know why he thought a prescription of booze for the depressed son of an alcoholic was the right thing to do but it worked. I can't remember what we talked about. The highball was sweet and quaffable and one hundred proof. I passed out. Somehow, they got me back to my mother's apartment and into bed. I woke up twenty-four hours later. I felt better but I knew I had to get away from Montreal.

Following on my father's logic, I decided Vancouver was the best place for me. I hadn't spoken to him since he left Montreal, but I decided to call him anyway. I told him I intended to spend a semester at Simon Fraser University and I wanted to live with him. And I did. Somehow my brush with my own version of his darkness made me want to be with him. I can't say I was motivated by a sense of duty or love. No, I was more desperate. I was acting on a survival instinct. I needed my father's help.

My father picked me up at the airport in a blue Ford Escort. He wore a blue suit with dandruff on the shoulders. His eyeglasses had a greasy film on the lenses and behind them his eyes were bloodshot. He was drinking again. On the drive to his apartment, he told me he had found a job as an *Encyclopedia Britannica* salesman. When I asked who he sold them to, he said, "Chinese families. They're all big on education." The clincher was the payment plan and the fact the encyclopedias came with a CD-ROM. "It has articles from all the top authorities in every field. Everything is at your fingertips. You could really use a set."

"Sure, I'll take one." As a child I had spent one summer reading from the set at my grandparents' farm. I was touched by the offer.

"All you have to do is give me enough money for the first monthly payment."

I didn't have the money. What I did have was the sinking feeling I shouldn't have come out to Vancouver. Aimee, who had turned eighteen a few months before, had already left my father and escaped back to Montreal, and I should have realized she left for a good reason. I asked him how Lenny was.

"He's running wild with a gang of boys."

I would soon learn that Lenny rarely came home and spent most nights staying with friends.

My father's rental townhouse had beige wall-to-wall carpet and no furniture. He used a bulk box of instant ramen noodles to prop up a television, and another served as a coffee table. I asked him where I could sleep. He poured himself a glass of whiskey, settled down on the floor, and pointed up the stairs. I found a spare bedroom with a futon mattress on the floor. I left my bags there and started back down the stairs. I could see my father pulling up another box of ramen to use as a headrest. I wanted to smash it over his skull. Instead I turned around and retreated to my new bedroom.

Moving in with my father was a terrible mistake. I planned my days so that I would be on campus from morning till ten at night. I would eat at the campus pub or, if I couldn't afford it, I wouldn't bother eating at all. I lived off my student loans and never asked him for any money. The few times that I caught him at home awake in front of the television, I would say, "Hey, Dad," but he was usually too drunk to respond. I would go straight to my room and read late into the night. If I heard the dead hiss of a TV station that had ended its broadcast day, I would go downstairs and turn the set off. There was always a blanket beside my father, which I would draw over him. He would rise early and leave before I could see him in the mornings. As for Lenny, there was hardly any sign of him. Things weren't the same as they had been at the cottage in Sainte-Adèle. He no longer needed me to take care of him. To my relief, weeks into my stay, Lenny too orchestrated his own return back to Montreal and resumed his life with my mother. I lasted four months with my father before I moved out.

That was the last time my father and I lived under the same roof. For the next ten years we lived no more than eight miles away from each other in the same city, and yet I saw him only once every year or two. I didn't want to see him anymore or watch his slow decline. He never did anything to change course. What's worse is I thought his failures were contagious. I feared if he was in my life he would drag me down with him. And so I spent the next decade pretending I no longer needed a father.

THE ARCHITECT FOR THE NEW SHOP CAME INTO
Modernize the other day to show Bill a plan for the
space. It is the size of a postage stamp. I asked Bill if I
could see the plans. On the ground floor there were only
four work stations.

"Will there be room for me?"

"Oh, sure," Bill said, and then he pointed to the second-
floor plan. Squeezed inside a storage room jammed with
shelves to hold bolts of fabric was a small rectangle representing a sewing machine. "You could sew there."

It was strange to see that drawing. On the one hand, they
had carved out a small space for me. On the other hand, it
was a marginal, tucked-away spot. I would be out of touch
with my master. I wouldn't be able to watch Park. I wouldn't
be able to progress. And, frankly, I would miss out on the
one thing I wanted most – their company. I needed to find
a way to make myself relevant to the shop and the shop
relevant to my pocketbook.

It's been a year since I first became Bill's apprentice. By now I thought I would be making coats or at least helping Bill and Park with alterations. I had hoped I would be ready to become a full-time paid employee of Modernize Tailors, but things haven't been going according to plan. I still haven't learned enough to tailor professionally. And then there's the matter of money to consider. To pay the bills, I've continued to file freelance fashion pieces. But there's always a price to be paid. Filing stories when I could be practising at the shop is preventing me from improving my skills. My apprenticeship has gone awry.

So I have a new plan. I've drawn the possible options for me at Modernize as an XY grid in my sketchbook. The X axis shows a range of income possibilities, ranging from my continuing to work for free to my earning a living wage. The Y axis covers the spectrum of likelihood, from the unlikely to the possible. In the highly lucrative but impossible corner of the grid is a box in which I've written *I am a tailor*. In the opposite corner, in the realm of the easily attainable but non-lucrative, I continue being Bill's unpaid apprentice.

The corner I like best represents the profitable and the possible. In the box there I've written in my perfect comic book penmanship, *What if we started a line of Modernize jeans?* We wouldn't even need to use a factory. I know I can make them. I've figured out the details. If I can make two pairs a day, each a custom fit, and I charge $300 a pair, I could make a living *and* continue training at the shop. And who knows, given enough time, maybe one day I could become a tailor.

But first I have to show the grid to Bill.

The trick is how to broach the subject. The shop is busy today, as it has been for the last few weeks. There's a buzz in the air. Everybody knows Modernize is going to move in the next few months and customers are rushing in to place their orders. But during a break in the early afternoon Bill waves me over to the cutting table.

"JJ, I want to talk to you about what's going to happen next."

"That's great, 'cause I wanted to show you something." I get my sketchbook out and flip to the page with my grid. "I've been trying to figure out what's possible and what's a good way for me to start earning money here so I can pay my keep." I start to walk him through my options at Modernize. Then he sees the square I've highlighted in yellow.

"How many times do I have to tell you we don't make jeans at Modernize?" He raps his hands against the top of the table. "You're not talking like an apprentice."

"I know, but if we make jeans I could generate revenue. I would be useful to the shop and it would buy me time. I can't do this for free anymore."

"That's what I'm saying. You need to do what's right for you. And I can't in good conscience let you waste your time here. Besides, there's no money in tailoring."

"You made a life for yourself here. Why can't I?"

"Tailoring is not for you. Maybe fashion design. You could go back to school. But here in the shop, it isn't right for you. It's okay if you want to come in once a week to practise, but we can't use you."

Bill is firing me and I don't know what I'm supposed to do next.

I will no longer be able to say Bill is my master, and though I know the appellation sounds antiquated, it matters to me. There will be no more pats on the back. There will be no more Bill. I'm on the outside looking in again. I've lost another home.

I can't look at him. I'm remembering all the times customers have stumbled over me at the machine at the front of the store as they come in and asked, "Are you Bill's son?" Each time I experienced the vicarious pleasure of the impostor who has lost himself in his disguise, almost believing it to be real. Then there was the greater pleasure I felt when Bill would put his hand on my shoulder and say with pride, "No, he's my apprentice."

But I'm not even good enough to be an apprentice.

"I'm doing you a favour," says Bill. "You have to think of your family." He moves his hands over the table as if he's wiping off crumbs or shuffling a deck of cards, dispersing what has been. The radio is on. A scissor clacks. There is a hiss of the iron. Jack is working at his machine; I can tell by the sound of the motor. Bill doesn't know how good he has it.

But, he's right: There's no future for me here. This isn't my home. And Bill can't replace my father.

Then I do the oddest thing. Throughout the conversation I've been playing with a scrap of flannel which I've folded and knotted in such a way that it looks like a flower. I put a pin through it. I give Bill the wool flower and I say, "Thank you." There is nothing left to say.

My face wet with tears, I clean up my work station. I pack my scissors into my bag along with the scraps I have been sewing. I grab my jacket, a blue blazer (though not my father's), and I pick off the threads that cling to it. Only a true tailor has the right to leave threads hanging on his coat. Bill and I shake hands. The chime on the door rings as I step out of the shop.

It is a bright afternoon and I walk to the Skytrain station. Once aboard I see a man in a three-button suit. All his buttons are fastened. I tell him it'll fit better if he loosens the bottom one.

"How would you know?"

I say, "Trust me."

It is sometimes hard to resist an encore, but a little tact will get you out of the difficulty, especially if you have studied, as every conjuror should do, the variation and combination of tricks. There are a score of different ways of vanishing a given article, and as many of reproducing it; and either one of the first may be used in conjunction with either of the second. Thus, by varying either the beginning or the end, you make the trick to some extent a new one.

Professor Louis Hoffmann, *Modern Magic*

I KEEP STICKING MY HAND INSIDE THE BREAST pocket of my father's suit in the hopes of finding something, a ticket stub, a business card, even a strand of his hair, just so I can have something more of him than this suit. Each time I find only lint and crumbs, and yet my hand returns to it again and again.

Of all the features in the landscape of the suit, the breast pocket is one of the most curious. Imagine if it were not there. Without the minimalist slash on the surface (finished with a tab of fabric called a welt), there would only be a dead zone between the lapel and the shoulder. The breast pocket relieves the eye. It makes a suit handsome. Angled correctly, it has the desirable effect of lifting and broadening the chest. Only the clumsy would make it dead flat and horizontal, which would visually widen the wearer's torso. No, it needs to rise towards the shoulder but ever so slightly. Set too acutely, it can make a chest look like it is caving in. The breast pocket sits just to the left of the left lapel. Sometimes, though rarely, it appears on the right side. Those who set a breast pocket on both sides (examples can be found) fail to recognize the inherent asymmetry of coats. Visually, the left side is always slightly larger than the right as a result of how men draw the left side of the coat over the right to button it up. The breast pocket helps restore balance.

It's best over the left. If a man feels the need to make a solemn pledge or to indicate mutely cardiovascular distress or convey a hammy gesture of thanks from the theatre stage, he might well place his right hand on his breast pocket, for beneath it beats his heart. Its proximity to the all-important organ, metabolically and symbolically – makes the breast pocket the psychic hotspot of the suit. It is there that a man will fly his colours and shelter things most precious to him. Surely, you say, not in the breast pocket? But indeed, yes, for the suit jacket has two pockets in collocation: the one everyone sees on the outside and the one that hides in the lining.

The inside pocket is obviously the more intimate keeping place. Passports, billfolds, heartfelt acceptance speeches, a gold-nibbed fountain pen, scrawled phone numbers of potential lovers – these belong tucked inside. Then, there are Bibles.

In his memoir of his visit to the Confederate South during the Civil War in the summer of 1862, an English reverend by the name of Malet wrote about meeting a "reckless" rebel captain who "said he would get a Bible the first opportunity, for he had heard say a Bible would stop a bullet; so after a battle he found one on a dead Yankee, and put it in his breast pocket, and in the next battle a ball hit the Bible, but did not penetrate to his body." Confederate troops were not the only ones saved by the Good Book. In the annual proceedings of the New York Bible Society in 1864, there are several accounts of how a Bible or a Testament in a breast pocket had saved a Northern Union soldier. The document also describes how Civil War infantry might have shown each other the inscriptions made in their Bibles by the people back home, much like how American GIs in the Second World War would pull out family pictures from their breast pockets. In other words, it was not only for its anti-ballistic properties that the Bible was placed inside breast pockets and treasured on the front lines.

One thing that rarely goes into a breast pocket anymore is a cigarette case. In Ian Fleming's *From Russia with Love*, James Bond is saved from a bullet by one. So is Noel Coward in the 1935 film *The Scoundrel*. Similarly, the nineteenth-century fairy tale "The Ducat and the Farthing" puts the whole trope in a medieval setting: a merciful sultan takes a measly farthing as ransom for a prisoner and drops the coin in his breast pocket. Later, in battle, the coin saves him from a lethal arrow wound. The story's moral is compassion begets compassion. What we keep in the inner pocket mirrors what we cherish in our hearts: the cigarette case echoes the premium one places on sophistication; a plane ticket is a yearning for escape or a return home; a comb soothes the vain; a photograph needs no explanation.

What can be said of items stored in the outside breast pocket? Anything held in it may be visible but it nevertheless still lies close to the heart. Architects who sketch often keep their pens there. The proud and bookish might keep their reading glasses on display. The exterior pocket is not quite a window into a man's soul. It is more like his front porch – a semi-private, semi-public platform. We put there things we do not mind for our neighbours to see.

Since around 2005, the practice of placing pocket squares, pocket puffs, or handkerchiefs in the breast pocket has crept back into the lexicon of male dress. Alan Flusser suggests one can make a silk kerchief puffed, plopped, furled, or twisted. He warns, though, "Folding a hank requires mindful care, like the tying of a bow tie, the most important thing to remember is that its deportment should appear unstudied, effortlessly contributing to the overall aplomb." Russell Smith, a Canadian menswear writer whom I admire, offers this fine advice: "Close your eyes and stuff it in."

I believe the only rules a sophisticated user of handkerchiefs should follow come from the world of magic. According to Professor Louis Hoffmann, author of *Modern Magic*, the first rule is, "Never tell your audience beforehand what you are going to do." The second is, "Never perform the same trick twice on the same evening." Hoffman explains that a trick loses "half its effect on repetition, but besides this, the audience knows precisely what is coming, and have all their faculties directed to find out at what point you cheated their eyes on the first occasion."

The first time one sees a man wearing a four-pointed pocket square it is hard not to notice how pleasing its effect

is, especially if it is white linen with hand-rolled edges in a contrasting colour like red or yellow. However, the decorative swatch – folded and ironed to form a quartet of triangular peaks – can wear out its welcome. The same goes for its cousin: the white linen ironed into a plain square. Its crispness is to be admired, but when worn every day it can come across as rigid and doctrinaire. In fact, tuxedo rental boutiques used to staple thin strips of linen onto rectangles of cardboard to create mock pocket squares to go with their velvet clip-on bow ties.

Like magicians (and pitchers for that matter), the pocket accessorizer needs to know when to change things up. As the day goes on, the confident man will not stress over his puff or square shifting a few degrees or even sinking below the welt-line. Why can't a pocket square be like a face, changing with moods, whimsy, and circumstances? A man with a permanently fixed half-smile would eventually be thought of as

WHY CAN'T A POCKET SQUARE BE LIKE A FACE, CHANGING WITH
MOODS, WHIMSY, AND CIRCUMSTANCES?

insincere, if not mad. So it goes with the pocket square. It requires only the flourish of the hand to give it new life, a new expression. A quick plunge into the pocket and a tug partly out, followed by a glance in the mirror, and the final manipulation is magical. A neatly folded square for the morning business meeting can be transformed into a scrunched rosette by happy hour. *Ta-da.*

So consider the interior pocket the place where one cultivates steadfastness while the exterior pocket is the stage for more mercurial expressions. How and what can be stuffed inside can be idiosyncratic and ad hoc. I say anything goes — flowers, a superhero figurine, a neck scarf — as long as it is true to the moment. Old-time TV pros used blank index cards in lieu of pocket squares. (I've tried it for TV interviews. It works. Even with high-definition cameras, you still can't tell the difference.) If you find yourself having to go out in the evening and your child is petulant, have him draw you a special dedicated picture. Tell him you will keep it with you all night long, close to your heart. Get him to fold the picture and place it in your breast pocket, and promise to tell everyone you meet who made it. No doubt, you will.

Some men won't wear pocket squares because they think they smack of the showman. They do. The handkerchief is one of the most basics props of the prestidigitator. It can be used to distract or make things disappear. Throw a handkerchief over something and your audience will immediately assume you are going to make the object go *poof.* It can also disguise delivery of the illicit. And besides being an important element in magic acts, a handkerchief does have practical applications. It is useful in staunching wounds, signalling surrender, and, according to the French Code of duelling, it can be used to strengthen and protect the wrist of a swordsman. If the duel is with pistols, a pair of silks can be laid out on the field to mark the distance at which opponents may fire on each other.

The outward wearing of fabric has its origin in gallantry. In the Middle Ages, a lover's handkerchief could find a place of honour on the armour of a knight: he would tie it underneath the plume of his helmet. The saying to wear one's heart on one's sleeve may have two possible origins. Knights sometimes wore their beloved's actual sleeves tied to their gauntlets (though I can't imagine how tearing portions of one's clothes off is romantic). Women often received handkerchiefs and gloves as gifts, and handkerchiefs were frequently tucked into their sleeves. Despite the contemporary hanky rule "one to show [breast pocket] and one to blow [back pants pocket]," there are circumstances where a pristine pocket square will be called up to service. At a funeral, unlike the functional rag in the back, an unused hanky can be shared, even given as a gift, at the teariest moment – a gesture that will never be forgotten.

My father did not wear pocket squares, but he did think of himself as a magician. For years, I thought he could literally detach the top of his thumb from the rest of his right hand. I never suspected the floating thumb belonged to his left hand. He also liked to pull quarters out from behind my ears. I never saw the coin in his hands before the reveal, but for some reason with this particular trick I knew it was there.

He once amazed me when I was maybe four or five with a full-blown disappearing trick. He made me sit at one end of the hall as he pulled a thin blanket off a bed and stood at the other end. My father held the blanket up as high to the ceiling as he could so all I could see of him were his knuckles at the top. Then he waved the blanket up and down. It fluttered. Suddenly he tossed it straight up into the air, where it hung suspended in space for a brief moment. When it fell to the floor, he was gone. I was astonished and scared. Then there was a knock at the front door. It was him.

My father must have been surprised by how well his improvised trick had gone because he attempted it again. Up again went the blanket, which floated in the air momentarily. But on this second try, through a space between the blanket and hallway wall, I could see him darting into the bedroom. I ran down the hall and saw his rear end scrambling to get through the window. It was strange to be caught between the thrill of the first act and the let-down of the second, but disappointment didn't displace the wonder. It left me wanting more.

THE LAST TIME I SAW MY FATHER WAS FOR THANKS-
giving. Melissa and I had invited him to join us for a holiday
meal. This was unusual. It was normal procedure to avoid
him and his phone calls when he was drinking. During his
last round of late-night calls, he complained about my mother
and how she was responsible for so much of what had happened and what a terrible job she had done raising his children. He also used to call me up to tell me he had a house and
a career when he was my age and how he should have sent
me to military school because I lacked discipline. It would
have done me good to live out on my own like he did when
he was thirteen. I would have developed a work ethic. Then
he would move on to complain about the blacks and the
Jews. I found his racist diatribes far more disturbing than his
litany of my shortcomings. At this point I would hang up.

But that year, Melissa and I decided to extend a last-
minute invitation. I could tell you our turkey was too big
for just the two of us and we would have never been able to

finish the leftovers in a week, but that would be flippant. I invited him out of guilt and longing. I still held out hope for my father. I wanted to see him.

When he arrived, I was surprised. No, I was ecstatic: my father was sober. We had a great meal. He talked about Joe Montana, I talked about John Elway. We faced off. He listed off the members of the 1976 Montreal Canadiens: Dryden, Lafleur, Robinson. I went through the roster of the 1986 Habs: Roy, Naslund, Lemieux. We argued over which Stanley Cup squad was more miraculous, though the evening itself was the true miracle.

I reverted to being a little boy. I hauled out of the hall closet a trio of old baseball gloves I had found at an antique store. One was an Al Kaline Wilson A-2204, featuring the Grip-Tite Pocket. The next was a Rawlings Reggie Jackson playground model. The one that caught my father's attention was the oldest: a Cooper Weeks Thin Line Little League. The burgundy leather was worn and puffy like a catcher's mitt. It had three fingers and a thumb. It was primitive.

"I'm teaching myself how to pitch," I said. A wistful look passed across his face. He got off the couch and picked up the old mitt with his meaty fingers. He put it on and punched it hard. Then he stared into the palm of the glove, at the point of impact. I told him I was sneaking into empty parkades and chucking hardballs against concrete walls. I told him I had a sinker, a pigeon ball that functioned as a curve, and a sidearm slider. But there was one problem: I didn't have a fastball.

He flapped the glove open and closed and punched the pocket one more time. "I used to pitch."

I never knew. "When did you pitch?"

"When I was a kid. I loved baseball."

There were questions I wanted to ask. *What was it like to be a pitcher when you were a boy? Why didn't you ever talk to me about baseball? What was it like to never know your mother? To be raised by your grandparents? Why do you never speak about the past?*

Throughout my life, my father never gave any hint that he might understand what it was like to be in my place. He never admitted that a son could be disappointed in his father. Would it have been so wrong for us to acknowledge we bore the same burdens? He should have given voice to his own sorrows with his father, and his grandfather. With himself. The truth wouldn't have made me more afraid than I already was, but perhaps I would have shown him more compassion.

Yes, I had questions.

But on this day, we decided to play baseball with each other. We walked down the street to the park, taking with us two gloves and a ball. When we got there, he checked the slope of the ground to make sure it simulated the standard drop from the mound to home plate. He picked out a good clearing and walked twenty-six paces downhill from me and turned around. Then he squatted down into a crouch and socked the glove one more time. He was ready to receive.

We fell into a quiet rhythm. I threw my side-arm concoction and the ball did indeed settle into my father's glove in avian style. My father sent the ball back with a throw that hung hard down. When I caught it, the ball was heavy, and stung. He crossed the distance between us and touched my wrist.

"Cock it like this." He gently bent my throwing hand back into a right angle. "It will come out faster." Then he walked back down and settled over an imaginary home plate.

For the first time in my life, we played catch. Instead of words we threw the ball back and forth between us, relishing the sure arc of the ball, the solid punctuation of each catch, and the assurance we would receive what the other had to deliver. If the ball was misthrown or skipped on by, a "sorry" was muttered. And that was nearly enough.

IT HAS BEEN MONTHS SINCE I'VE BEEN TO THE SHOP. I continue to do the alterations to my father's suit in my spare time, between writing fashion columns. When I settle down to tackle the suit, I remember the little tricks and techniques Bill and the tailors tried to teach me. I do my best but I'm not tortured by my mistakes. I'm not sure I will ever wear this suit out of the apartment, but suddenly I feel free to do what I wish.

I have decided to sew the buttons back on. I made the decision after rereading *Complexity and Contradiction in Architecture*, written in 1966 by the architect Robert Venturi. In it, Venturi launched an attack on the monolith of modern architecture. What he bemoaned was the monotonous simplification of form. New buildings at the time had been so reduced to their essentials, so denuded of decoration and historical references to earlier forms, that they had become dead boring. Many didn't even meet functional demands: modern buildings couldn't prevent the sun from overheating rooms or keep people warm in the winter.

Venturi argued the architectural idiom could be deeper, richer, and more capable of handling complexity than the modernists supposed. He pointed to Mannerist architects like Michelangelo who incorporated functional yet decorative elements like arches and pediments into the facade of a building where none was structurally required. Venturi called this idea of mixing form and function, of not being a slave to pure function, and of using decoration for its own sake, the "Phenomenon of Both-And": a building detail could be "both good and awkward, big and little, closed and open, continuous and articulated, round and square, structural and spatial. An architecture which includes varying levels of meaning breeds ambiguity and tension."

My father's suit can be my Mannerist edifice. It will remain Both-And. It doesn't have to be perfect, it just has to be something of my father that is also for me.

I suppose the punk is still in me because I don't care if I can't wear it for a job interview. Besides, do I really want a job I could get only by wearing a suit? I don't want to follow the rules of pattern-making, of suit-wearing etiquette, of fashion how-to's anymore. I don't need rules.

In fact, I'm wondering if in those early days my father tried too hard. He tried to be rich. He tried to be successful. He tried to check every little box there was to check off, and it only led him further away from us, from me, and from being happy with himself. In attempting to achieve everything, he left us with nothing. I won't make the same mistake.

I have decided the suit will be fun, young, heedless. Maybe even impolite, with an "exposed beam" look on the front? No, cross that. I'm going to leave the pants just the way they are. The jacket will be tight on the top, the pants will be loose and long.

Okay, maybe I am too old for another adolescent fashion rebellion, but I remember what a fortune cookie once told me: "Don't delay, do what you do best."

The brass buttons are flashy. Fine. I'm flashy.

Next I decide to attack the side seams. My father had four or five inches over me in the belly. If I take off four inches from the side seams, the hem of the coat will flare, but I remind myself I am no longer searching for absolute perfection. I go at the side seams from the outside, using the ladder stitch David Wilkes showed me. It works nearly as well as if I had sewn it from the inside like a good tailor is supposed to. But then, I'm not a good tailor, am I?

The new Modernize is off to the left of the lobby and locked behind a gate. There's a buzzer. Through the glass door, I see Bill. He looks older and thinner. He stoops a little bit more. Has it been that long?

"Oh, my apprentice," he says, without sarcasm.

"How have you been, Bill?"

"Can't complain. Busier than ever." He puts one hand on his hip and waves at a rack full of orders. Park, as usual, is leaning over a coat at the workbench. He glances up at me and then goes back to work. Some things never change. It's good to see him.

As the plans were drawn, the new shop is the size of a closet. But Bill wants to show me the upstairs storeroom.

"See, it's waiting for you." In the centre of the room is my sewing machine. I work the foot control. It feels too light.

"You fired me."

"Well, it was for your own good."

I thought relocating the shop would be a disaster, but I see now I was wrong and I'm thankful for it. Modernize is thriving. Bill is happy and healthy, and I'm relieved.

Back downstairs, we sit at the old order table in the lobby of the building. The shop has already spilled out of its confines and is in the process of taking over the entire ground floor. The change room is now a screened-off area in the corner. A new mirror hangs on another wall. A dressing dummy takes up space right in the middle of the lobby. Tenants with suites in the upper floors have to pick their way through it all. Nobody seems to mind.

As Bill eats his lunch, I find my old chair and pull it up to the table. Out of habit, I flip through the order sheets. It's like I never left.

"Some of these jobs have been done for weeks."

"Oh, really?"

"Do you want me to call them?"

"You don't have to anymore."

I tell him there's nothing else I would rather do and a sadness grips me as I realize I mean every word. But I also know this life isn't for me.

After Bill fired me, I met a Modernize customer named Robert Chaplin. Bill had made him a suit before I started working at the shop. It was for a special occasion. Chaplin had worn it in a chess match against former World Chess Champion Garry Kasparov. Chaplin was no grandmaster; in fact, he was a visual artist. He had created a chessboard out of Lego that Kasparov wanted, so Chaplin made him a deal: Kasparov could have the chessboard for free if Kasparov agreed to play one game with him. Chaplin made a rendez-vous with the chess champion in Toronto, girded in his Modernize suit, and lost in a quick seven moves.

I asked Chaplin about his experience at Modernize. Did he come into the shop with an image, a look, or a style in mind?

"No, man," he answered. "Bill is like Kasparov. He's a master. You have to give in to the process. They're artists practising a fine art. Once you step in there, you let them do their thing. That's their domain. It's like Zen."

What Chaplin said struck home. I never gave myself over fully to the process as an apprentice the way I should have. It wasn't all a loss, though. I have a feel for clothes now I didn't have before. I'm not talking about matters of style, I mean an understanding of the artifact, the garment itself. I don't look at clothes so much as I touch them now. If someone asks me what I think of their suit they better be prepared to be groped. What had been book knowledge is now embedded in my hands. Not as deeply as Bill's, of course, but it's there. Good touch.

When the phone rings, I turn to Bill and he nods. I pick up the receiver.

"Hello, Modernize Tailors, dressing the modern man since 1913. How may I help you?"

IN AUGUST 2001, TEN MONTHS AFTER MY FATHER and I played baseball in the park, I received a phone call from my mother.

"Your father is gone."

Had he gone back to China? My father had always fostered the fantasy of a prodigal's return. Maybe he finally made the leap. "Gone where?"

"He passed away."

"What are you talking about?"

"He's dead."

"What? I don't know what you mean."

"He's kaput." My mother has many faults, but her bluntness is not one of them. "*Ah-Be*, I'm so sorry."

I called the police. They told me he died on the bathroom floor in his ground-level apartment suite. The coroner said the cause was sepsis, blood poisoning by bacteria, which led to a heart attack. The medical examiner found lesions on his legs, which may have been the source of his blood infection. His alcoholism may also have been a factor as it had weakened his immune system.

Lenny flew in from Calgary. My mother and sisters flew in from Montreal. After gathering at my apartment we made our way to my father's place, which was only twenty minutes away, in the suburb next to mine. It would be my first visit there. The suite was dark and held the stale, close air of a smoker's home. The first room I looked in was the washroom. I half-expected to see his body still lying there. Instead I found only rubbish from the paramedics' efforts: ribbons of EKG paper, a latex glove, and wax paper wrappers. In the kitchen, a dozen empty bottles of blended whiskey sat under the sink. Dirty pots covered the counters. Grease made the stovetop tacky. We threw stained linens, pillows, unwashed dishes, and rotting food into large orange garbage bags. I found in a file folder my report cards from elementary school.

My mother set herself upon his closet, repeating the slow, dull sound of the hangers sliding across the metal rod and terminating with a click. One grey flannel jacket. A brittle, yellow hopsack sports coat made from a bolt of silk and linen. A heavy, distressed leather jacket. She stopped when she found the blue suit. She held it up and smoothed the front, stroking it. She said, "We need socks, shoes, and a tie."

At the funeral home, my mother and I walked up the stairs and followed the marble wall. The funeral director wanted to talk to us about our plans for an open casket. Apparently my father's body was showing advanced decomposition. It had something to do with what killed him. My mother and I still wanted to see his body. We told the funeral director it was our preference to dress him regardless of the state of his corpse. She asked us to follow her and led us around the corner. My mother held tight to the shopping bag with my father's suit in it.

"Mum, I want to do it."

"I know how to tie a tie. You think I'm an idiot?"

"Let me do it."

"You think you can tie a tie better than I can?" My mother was in full dragon lady mode.

"No. I just want to do it."

The funeral director led us down a dark hall where, though it was early August, the air was chilly. We stepped through a double doorway into a room that had the trappings of a canning room. It had a rustic feel, with jars lined along wood shelves. In the centre of the room, on a giant porcelain embalming table, lay my father, John Hing Foon Lee, age fifty-two.

His skin was matte and dun coloured. It was then I realized how it is the undertone of living blood flowing beneath the surface of our skin that gives our flesh its luminescence. When the blood no longer flows, skin loses its inner light. His skin looked like it had rusted or oxidized. It sagged away from his head to reveal the bone structure that had been hidden by his chubby cheeks. Now, he looked gaunt, ninety years old, lifeless. In life, he had always been bigger than me, but now he had become small. Trying to slip on his suit would have tested the resiliency of his flesh and joints.

In the end, we went with a closed casket. My mother wanted no eulogy and no one present but family. There would be no priest or prayers. No tie, no blue blazer suit. It had nothing to do with the state of his body, and everything to do with the state of our emotions. We wanted him to ourselves. Any song and dance would have angered us. In a way our lack of ceremony underscored how we didn't have any reliable structures by which to grieve or celebrate the good and the bad in our lives. We were still on our own.

My father went into a plywood box. Later in the day the family gathered in the funeral home chapel. I wore the grey ghillie suit, the one I would be too ashamed to wear again for my graduation a few months later. A white sheet was draped over the box with my father in it. My mother told us to bow to him three times and say goodbye. I stood up and bowed once before I broke down in tears. I cried not just for the loss of the man he was but the man he should have been. I cried because of all that was left unsaid and unknown. I cried because I still could not forgive him.

That's how I inherited my father's suit.

⚓

It was a month before I could bear to collect my father's ashes from the funeral home. They came in a small, tightly sealed box no larger than a Concise Oxford Dictionary. In October, two months after his death, Melissa and I flew to Montreal with them in my carry-on luggage. It was an odd package to carry so soon after the attack on the World Trade Center. I was worried people would think it was a bomb but it set off no alarms.

We drove with my mother and my sisters to Mount

Royal Cemetery. My great-grandparents were buried there. The ground was too hard for my father's grave but I wanted to see where his ashes would be interred. I wanted to be buried there too.

As a child I always thought it was a special honour to have my family's graves near the summit of the mountain. Their resting places were located higher up than those of the soldiers who fought in the First and Second World Wars, higher up than those of the Jews. I thought we must be special because we were near the very top. But as we made our way up with my father's ashes in my hands, I felt the cold and realized it was one of the worst parts of the mountain. A naked wind swept in from the east and cut through my coat. Erosion was eating away at the slopes, threatening the plots. My father's grave would be dug in a harsh hill where flower stems could be snapped by a single gust. This was the Chinamen's cemetery. The place to bury the people no one really wanted around. There was only one more spot beside my father.

I'm NOT SURE WHAT YOU WOULD THINK IF YOU SAW me in my father's suit. I would like you to think that I cut an elegant figure. It would be great if you thought I looked comfortable and wore it so effortlessly that I could be nothing less than a suit-wearing kind of man. If I gave off a whiff of desperation instead of an air of debonair, I would be disappointed. I would rather be keen and bright than preening and pompous. Indomitable would be preferred to overblown and insecure. But I think I am chasing what can't be caught.

In truth, I still don't know what makes for a good suit. I mean I can tell you if a suit is well made and it fits you, and whether the cut and style are current. What I can't tell you is how that suit will behave in the wild, out there on the streets, across the candlelit table, at the wedding chapel, in the dock or the boardroom.

When I look again at that picture of my father, my uncle, and my great-grandfather in Sherbrooke, Quebec in the late

1950s, I see they are not very well dressed, but I like this picture a lot because it captures the intergenerational nature of the suit. It is something passed on from one generation to the next. And the knowledge passed down was a code. Ostensibly it was about knots and sleeve lengths and which buttons to close and which to leave open, but in reality what was shared was an acknowledgement: Son, you're going to need this one day, maybe not right now, but one day.

Most fathers will know nothing about the martial origins of the suit or how its lines have an uncanny resemblance to plate armour. Fathers won't be able to tell you the most masculine article in a man's sartorial arsenal comes alive with the feminine unrolling of the lapel. They won't be able to tell you how suits are contradictions. And it won't really matter.

I look at the photo of my father at the Kon-Tiki one more time. He is only twenty-one years old. This is before he became an alcoholic, before he suffered from massive depression, and decades before he died. My father is elegant, effortless, debonair, pompous, overblown, and achingly too young. I look at the picture and he remains an enigma.

꒐

My father's arms reach around me. His sleeves are rolled. He hunches so his face hovers over my shoulder, right next to mine. This is our second try.

"Okay, now you loop it over on one side."

"Like this?"

"Yes, that's right. That's what makes it a half-Windsor."

"I look like you, now."

"One day, you might. Just practise it and you can use it on important days. When you have to wear a suit like Daddy."

"Why?"

"Because I want you to be ready."

"Ready for what?"

"Anything, son."

IN FRONT OF THE FULL-LENGTH MIRROR I TELL myself, "I'm finished."

"What?"

Jack is playing with a pair of die-cast jet fighters on the bed. He's lying down with his arms in the air. The German multi-purpose Tornado is the size of a Canadian dollar coin. He makes a loop to lose the French Mirage on its tail.

Jack is husky and smooth-skinned. He likes his pants cut wide. He is easy going, but when he was born his face was scrunched into red angry folds and he would not stop crying. He lost so much weight in the first week I thought he would die. At night he would stick out his tongue and make it quaver with a ceaseless wail. Because she knows it was never true, Melissa likes to remind me that, in a moment of frustration, I once said, "I will never be able to love him."

And I was wrong. When he sits in my lap I want time to stop. He thinks I patch the knees on his pants because it makes him look cool and not because we can't afford to buy new pants. Jack is the one who asked me to dress him in a bow tie for his first Christmas concert. It's easy to love him and it is easy to believe he'll love me forever. Jack purses his lips and unleashes a salvo of cannon fire made of onomatopoeia and spit.

"Weren't you listening?" says Emmet. "He said he finished the suit."

Emmet is also on the bed, lying beside his twin, but he's reading a Japanese comic book. It's about a phoenix. Those who drink its blood will live forever. Emmet is smaller and wiry. He likes to draw pictures of princesses and insists I alter all his jeans so they cling skintight. He is wild and iron-willed. He makes me work for his love and I do what I can to earn it.

Emmet glances up from the pages of his comic book. "You look good."

"Yeah, it looks nice," says Jack. Then he stops his air battle. "Daddy, when you die can I have it?"

"What?"

"The jacket. It looks nice."

"It was your grandfather's. Your daddy's daddy."

"I know. That's why I'm asking."

Emmet says, "If your daddy was alive, would you play with him?"

"I'm not sure what grown sons and fathers are supposed to do. I guess you talk about things."

"Will you still be our daddy when we grow up?"

"I'll always be your daddy. That will never change."

"Hey, can I have your ties?" says Emmet.

"Sure, you can. But can I hold onto these things for a while? You can have them when I die."

Jack says, "I don't want you to die. Ever."

"We all die some time. But I'll try not to. I want to live for a long time. I want to see you get old and then I want to die before you. Because the saddest thing is when a child dies before his mummy or daddy. Is that okay?"

"You'll wait until I'm old?"

"I'll do my very best."

"Okay."

Emmet says, "Why do you wear suits? Why do you even have to dress fancy?"

"Sometimes you dress fancy so you can feel good about yourself, and sometimes you do it so other people feel good about you and they don't worry about you."

"Will you teach me how to tie a tie?" says Emmet.

"When you learn how to tie your shoelaces, I'll show you. How about that, boys?"

"Even bow ties."

"Yes."

"Okay. Can we wrestle now?"

"In a second," I tell them. They tumble out of the room.

I know what I've said isn't true. There's more work to be done. The lapel stitches are uneven. I could shave another inch off the shoulders. The waist could be tighter. I can see in the suit all its shortcomings, its deficiencies. It is incomplete, but he's still there and now so am I. At this moment, I am occupying the same space as my father. We remain entangled.

The suit brought me here but I no longer need it to remember. He is back with me now. The forgetting has stopped, and

I don't want to forget anymore. I accept there may never be a day when all the pieces will be drawn together and I will see the whole. I don't need to judge him anymore. Or know his moral height or spiritual girth. I don't need to measure myself against him.

I take the jacket off and hold it to my face. After all the steam and tears and cuts and pricked fingers and knotted loose threads, the scent lingers, if only in my imagination — cigarettes, sweat, vanilla, him.

AUTHOR'S NOTE

This book, like a good suit, required a great deal of steaming, ironing, stretching, and gathering to make an acceptable whole. To achieve narrative coherence, I have taken certain liberties. For example, since 2006, I have attempted to alter my father's suit numerous times. All of them were abortive or tentative until I gritted my teeth and went for it with gusto in 2010. For dramatic purposes, I have synthesized all past efforts to read as one prolonged campaign.

Though my studies with Bill Wong occurred in 2006 and 2007 (and were documented as a tangent in the excellent 2008 film about Bill's life, *Tailor Made*, by director Len Lee and producer and co-director Marsha Newberry), I've taken certain liberties with the timeline for narrative flow. These helped to organize the memories of my childhood and of my father, and the memories of my time with Bill. As a side effect, strange, wonderful, and revelatory anachronisms pop up in this memoir. I find them felicitous, and as this book is about unity and bringing the past, present, and

[287]

future together, I felt no need to correct or suppress them.

Finally, after writing the final draft, I discovered that certain moments as I recalled them did not occur in the sequence I remembered. Quite a shock. But because I had taken them as truths for so long, and the misremembered had motivated my past actions and inform my understanding of my life, I have left them unrevised. Memory, it would seem, is its own tailor.

ACKNOWLEDGEMENTS

This book would not have happened without my editor, Anita Chong, book designer CS Richardson, and the people of McClelland & Stewart. Anita reached out to me in the dying days of CBC Radio's *Sounds Like Canada* with Shelagh Rogers, where I worked as an associate producer in 2008. The show was an iconic network program with an impending cancellation date, and I was at a loss as to how to carry on without it. Then out of nowhere, Anita called. She told me she had just heard my feature-length radio documentary, *The Measure of a Man*, on the CBC Radio's *Ideas*. Would I be interested, she wondered, in writing a book based on it?

Initially, I said, "No." I felt I had said all that I needed to say about suits in the documentary and in my work as a fashion columnist for the *Vancouver Sun* and CBC Radio's *On the Coast*.

But then, a few months later, I started looking for work. I found my hand skipping over my father's suit as I flicked through the hangers in my closet, picking clothes to wear during my job search. Then there was that scent.

It was a scent I had described in the radio documentary, and once again it fired my synapses. I called Anita, and so began a long personal journey exploring these memories of my father.

So, thank you, Anita, for bringing me closer to my memories and to him.

I am also grateful to CBC radio producer Kathleen Flaherty, who helped shepherd the radio version of this foray. It was Kathleen who said, when I still thought *The Measure of a Man* concerned itself with only fashion, "This doc is really about fathers." I didn't understand what she meant at the time, but I do now. Kathleen, you're the best.

I also wish to thank Bill Wong, Jack Wong, and all the men of Modernize Tailors. They are all great teachers and exceedingly kind souls.

CBC producers Karen Burgess, Phillip Ditchburn, Theresa Duvall, Yvonne Gall, Laura Palmer, Anne Penman, and Cathy Simon are all dear to me for allowing me to be a journalist who always got involved in the story — and to break nearly all the rules.

Thanks also to Charlie Smith, editor-in-chief of the *Georgia Straight*, and Juanita Ng of the *Vancouver Sun*, for letting my cock-eyed view of fashion grace their newsprint pages.

Thanks to William Skinner of Dege & Skinner; tailors Paul Frearson and Rory Duffy of Henry Poole & Company; tailor errant David Wilkes; Andrew Bolton, curator of the Costume Institute at the Metropolitan Museum; fashion designer and writer Alan Flusser; and historian Anne

Hollander: for spending beautiful late-autumn days in London, Vancouver, and New York with me, and sharing their knowledge of suits; they have my gratitude.

My final and deepest thanks go to my mother and siblings, and, of course, my wife, Melissa, who marshalled our meagre resources so I could write over the last two years. It was not easy, and she did this out of love and hope for better days to come. I love you and the boys. I couldn't have done anything without you.

⌂

The following books have a special place on my shelf and I recommend them for further reading:

Angeloni, Umberto. *The Boutonniere: Style in One's Lapel.* New York: Universe, 2000.

Chenoune, Farid. *A History of Men's Fashion.* Paris: Flammarion, 1993.

Edward VIII, the Duke of Windsor, *A Family Album.* London: Cassell & Company, 1960.

Flusser, Alan. *Dressing the Man: Mastering the Art of Permanent Fashion.* New York: HarperCollins, 2002.

Hollander, Anne. *Sex and Suits: The Evolution of Modern Dress.* New York: A.A. Knopf, 1994.

Martin, Richard, and Harold Koda. *Jocks and Nerds: Men's Style in the Twentieth Century.* New York: Rizzoli, 1989.

de Marly, Diana. *Fashion for Men: An Illustrated History.* London: B.T. Batsford, 1985.

Smith, Russell. *Men's Style: The Thinking Man's Guide to Dress.* Toronto: McClelland & Stewart, 2007.

Wherever possible, I have tried to acknowledge within the text the original source material for the quotations that appear throughout the book. For the reader's reference, here are a few additional acknowledgements.

The lyrics on p. 84 are from the traditional folk song "The Water Is Wide."

William Thourlby's quotation on p. 112 is from Thourlby's *You Are What You Wear* (New York: Forbes/Wittenburg & Brown, 1990).

The Beau Brummell quotations come from three main sources: William Jesse, *The Life of George Brummell, Esq., Commonly Called Beau Brummell* (London: J.C. Nimmo, 1886); Grace and Philip Wharton, *The Wits and Beaux of Society* (New York: Harper & Brothers, 1861); and William Russell, *Eccentric Personages* (John Maxwell and Company, 1864).

The quotations from Suzie Mackenzie's profile of Giorgio Armani on pages 160-61 are from the article "The Gentle Touch," *The Guardian*, December 11, 2004.

The epigraph on p. 171 is from H.J. Chappell's "Salesmanship for Tailors," as cited in A.S. Bridgland (ed.), *The Modern Tailor, Outfitter, and Clothier* (London: Caxton, 1928), vol. 2.

The quotation on p. 187 is from Yugen Matsumura, as cited in Dorinne Kondo's *About Face: Performing Race in Fashion and Theater* (New York: Routledge, 1997).

My illustrations of historical figures were adapted from the
following sources.

66:      Charles II, after an etching by Coryn or Quirin Bol
(Boel), 1660s, National Portrait Gallery.

115:     Beau Brummell, after a watercolour by Richard
Dighton, 1805.

159:     Armani sportscoat, after a still of Richard Gere
from the film *American Gigolo*, 1980.

188-89: Samurai of Chōshō and Satsuma in Western dress,
after photographs by Felice Beato, ca. 1870.

214:     Oscar Wilde, after a photograph by Napoleon
Sarony, 1882.

241:     Edward, Duke of Windsor, then Prince of Wales,
after a royal family photograph published by *Life*,
June 5, 1950.

A NOTE ABOUT THE TYPE

The Measure of a Man is set in Joanna, designed in 1930 by Eric Gill and released by the Monotype Corporation in 1937. Gill created the typeface for the firm of Hague & Gill (a printing company he founded in order to give his son-in-law an occupation). Reminiscent of Gill's earlier designs for the faces Perpetua and Cockerel, Joanna is, as he described it, "a book face free from all the fancy business." It is named for one of Gill's daughters.

BOOK DESIGN BY CS RICHARDSON